ADHD TOOLS FOR COUPLES

The 8 Techniques We Use To Create Love, Stability And Understanding In Our ADHD Relationship

Copyright © 2023 by LearnWell Books.

All rights reserved. No part of this publication may be reproduced, distributed, or transmitted in any form or by any means, including photocopying, recording, or other electronic or mechanical methods, without the prior written permission of the publisher, except in the case of brief quotations embodied in critical reviews and certain other noncommercial uses permitted by copyright law.

References to historical events, real people, or real places are often fictitious. In such cases, the names, characters, and places are products of the author's imagination. We do this where it's important to protect the privacy of people, places, and things.

689 Burke Rd
Camberwell Victoria 3124
Australia

www.LearnWellBooks.com

We're led by God. Our business is also committed to supporting kids' charities. At the time of printing, we have donated well over $100,000 to enable mentoring services for underprivileged children. By choosing our books, you are helping children who desperately need it. Thank you.

This is really important.
It's a sincere thank you.

My name is Wayne, the founder of LearnWell.

My Dad put a book in my hands when I was 13. It was written by Zig Ziglar and it changed the course of my life. Since then, it's been books that have helped me get over breakups, learn how to be a good friend, study the lives of good people and books have been the source of my persistence through some pretty challenging times.

My purpose is now to return the favor. To create books that might be the turning point in the lives of people around the world, just like they've been for me. It's enough to almost bring me to tears to think of you holding this book, seeking information and wisdom from something that I've helped to create. I'm moved in a way that I can't fully explain.

We're a small and 'beyond-enthusiastic' team here at LearnWell. We're writers, editors, researchers, designers, formatters (oh ... and a bookkeeper!) who take your decision to learn with us incredibly seriously. We consider it a privilege to be part of your learning journey. Thank you for allowing us to join you.

If there's anything we did really well, anything we messed up, or anything AT ALL that we could do better, would you please write to us and tell us (like, right now!) We would love to hear from you!

readers@learnwellbooks.com

We're sending you our thanks, our love and our very best wishes.

Wayne

and the team at LearnWell Books.

WELCOME TO OUR COMMUNITY

"It's like a private online book club"

Imagine if you could actually meet and talk with other readers of this book and share your experiences.

Imagine if you could chat with the author or join them on a live Q&A!

Imagine getting access to the author's notes and other exclusive, unpublished material.

You can do all of that and a lot more in the LearnWell Online Community!!

→ Download your **Workbook**
→ Chat directly with the author!
→ Meet and feel supported by other readers and their experiences.
→ Access additional, exclusive content about this topic and others.
→ Join our live Author Q&A sessions online.
→ Learn faster, make lasting changes, and have 10 times more fun!

All of this is part of our commitment to creating the best learning resources in the world.

Scan the QR code to get FREE access
www.learnwellbooks.com/foundthekeys

CONTENTS

	Introduction	8
1	Love Always Starts With Understanding What ADHD Is And How It Affects Us?	10
2	Common Challenges and Proven Coping Strategies The Things We All Go Through	29
3	Wait. What Was I Saying? How To Establish Effective Communication Between You	43
4	Where Did The Time Go? And Where Are My Keys? Managing Time And Being (More) Organized	62
5	Everyone Take A Deep Breath! How To Regulate The Emotional ourney Of ADHD	73
6	It's Your Turn To Do The Dishes Managing The Chores Without One Person Doing It All	83
7	Wait. You Bought What?! Effective Money Management	94

8	**Not Tonight, Babe**	104
	Enhancing Your Intimacy And Sexuality	
9	**Creating A Brilliant Relationship**	118
	Strategies To Thrive Despite The Challenges	

References   125

YOUR WORKBOOK

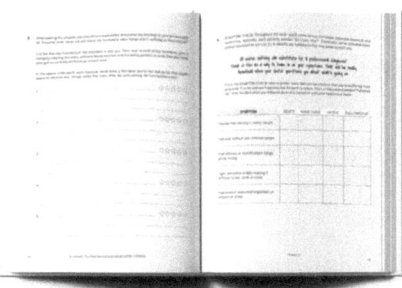

A shocking truth was discovered by a study done in 1987 – **people only remember 10% of what they read!**

That seems so discouraging.

But here's the **GOOD NEWS** – reading is **NEVER** a waste of time. As long as you do **one** important thing ...

The same study (by National Training Laboratories) shows that you will remember 90% of what you read when you **put your new knowledge into action**!

Here at LearnWell, we aim to create **the world's best learning resources**. So, we have included a highly engaging **Workbook** that helps you put your new knowledge into fun, practical action.

So, make sure you download your **FREE Workbook.** You'll find it located inside the **LearnWell Community.** Simply scan the QR code below for access.

Get your Workbook in the LearnWell Community
Scan the QR Code for access or go to:
www.learnwellbooks.com/foundthekeys

INTRODUCTION

Navigating the challenges of ADHD as a couple can be emotionally painful, time-consuming, and extremely frustrating. Millions of couples face the complexities of a relationship where ADHD is present. This means they'll be dealing with communication breakdowns, financial stress, and emotional detachment. However, there are transformative actions that can make a real difference. How do I know? Because I've personally experienced the very same struggles. Perhaps the same struggles that brought you to this book.

Initially, my partner Sally and I had a strong relationship, but over time, ADHD began to erode our loving connection. The pain and frustration of this led me to breaking point, where I had the choice of staying and developing a better understanding or leaving forever. I decided to stay. I fought for us. It involved years of research, therapy, trials and much error but from my rock-bottom moment to today, I have discovered what it takes to make a relationship like this work. And now, I want to guide you through all of the lessons that I had to learn to save the love of my life.

Within the pages of this comprehensive and compassionate guide, you'll read our uncensored stories of the highs and lows we endured, the lessons they produced and the actions that we took that kept us together. This will equip you with the knowledge you need to heal your own relationship. Together, we'll explore effective communication techniques, financial strategies, and other invaluable tools to alleviate the burdens of living with ADHD.

Ignoring the issue won't make it disappear; you must actively confront it.

I'll demask the common misconceptions of this condition and uncover genuine solutions. You'll gain a deep understanding of how ADHD impacts your relationship and, most importantly, how to effectively address these challenges. I can personally vouch for the effectiveness of these methods, as they transformed my life and dissolved many misunderstandings that plagued our journey as a couple.

I'll also vouch for the LearnWell Community as a valuable support for this journey

I promise that reading this book will provide you
with a fresh perspective on the issues you've been grappling with. Through its pages, you'll acquire the knowledge and strategies necessary to combat ADHD and prevent it from further disrupting your life. It's time to reclaim the love that lies within your relationship and build a future of harmony and understanding.

LOVE ALWAYS STARTS WITH UNDERSTANDING

What ADHD Is And How It Affects Us?

You don't love someone because they're perfect, you love them in spite of the fact that they're not.

– Jodi Picoult

He glanced over his shoulder for one last look down the corridor and thought about what might have been. This could have been perfect. It *had* been perfect for a while. Yet, something had come between them and ruined the relationship. If only they'd known how to make it work.

He shook his head as the door slowly swung closed behind him, ending their time together with questions rather than answers and those questions would now remain unanswered. He sighed and headed out into the cold new day, trying to think of it as a fresh start rather than the bitter end.

How do I know all this happened? Because the person closing that door was me.

And the person on the other side? My partner that I'd loved but failed to fully understand.

The thing that had come between us? ADHD, or attention-deficit/hyperactivity disorder.

If I'd known then what I know now, maybe that door would have stayed open. But like so many people, I didn't understand the destructive impact that ADHD can have on relationships. I just didn't know that we should have been fighting a common enemy instead of each other.

I guess we all make mistakes. We all learn things too late in life to make a difference. Ours was an unfortunate imitation of so many millions of other cases where couples have tried, fought and lost against ADHD.

Perhaps you're reading this because you're worried. Just like I was. You're worried that there's something wrong with you. Or, you may be blaming the relationship. Maybe one of you has been diagnosed with ADHD, or maybe you've seen issues that make you suspect ADHD could be a feature in your relationship, and it's causing turbulence.

A few days - or maybe it was a few weeks - after closing that door I started thinking more deeply about what had happened. What was it that had caused us to drift apart? We'd been great together for the first few months. Walking hand in hand in the sunlight. Laughing at each other's silly jokes while the world around us faded into the background. All the usual things you've seen a hundred times in corny, romantic films.

Then little things started to irritate me. Nothing major at first, just niggling little things like the way she would forget things she'd promised to do. Or how she'd leave things lying around.

It was actually a running joke between us at first. When you're young and in love, even the problems can seem cute and endearing. But things got a lot more serious when we started living together. Suddenly, all the chores she forgot to do or the items she left lying about had more serious consequences. I started to get short-tempered, and that made the situation worse.

LIVING TOGETHER. HER, ME AND ADHD

I'm quite an organized person and I hate seeing a mess around the house. Or being left out in the rain because someone forgot what time they were meant to meet me. That one night was awful. I eventually arrived home with water running down my face, dripping off my nose. She was lying on the sofa half-watching some stupid reality show I hated.

"Oh, you're all wet!"

"I know."

"You should have taken an umbrella!"

"I didn't expect to be standing in a tropical monsoon at the bus stop for an hour."

"You should have just got on a bus then. What were you waiting for?"

The look of confusion in her dark eyes when I lost my temper. The feel of the shirt sticking to my back and my feet squelching in my wet shoes. Those are the kind of experiences I just couldn't overlook.

So, I left. One day when I realized that I couldn't see any light at the end of this long, emotional tunnel. I felt like I was going crazy and needed some space.

As I said, a few days or weeks later I started picking over this failed relationship in my mind. I could try to pretend that I was looking for ways to develop as a person, to 'grow from all this'. But really, I wanted to find ways to blame it all on her. I had tried my best to make the relationship work while she seemed to just coast through it all without making much of an effort. I was the good guy here. She didn't even bother trying. Wasn't that the problem?

I was sufficiently satisfied with that explanation. Until the day I read about something called ADHD. Sure, I'd heard about it before. But doesn't it only affect kids when they have too much sugar or something? I forgot about it until another person's story caught my eye and I kept reading.

You're here because something in my story sounds similar to your own. That's exactly how I started. And it changed my life.

Let's take a few steps backwards so we can explore some of the technical aspects of this condition.

ADHD is a type of neurodevelopmental disorder. It can cause trouble in many areas of life, from not paying attention to being too impulsive or incredibly restless.

You normally hear people talking about ADHD in kids. While the theories about it being caused by too much sugar or orange juice haven't been clearly proven, it's still seen as mainly a problem for young people. One of the most common comments people make is that "they'll grow out of it". And sure, in a lot of cases ADHD turns into a sort of vague restlessness that the person can disguise more easily as they grow up.

But not everyone grows out of it and many people go through life without ever getting a proper ADHD diagnosis.

The first mention of this condition came at the start of the 20th century[1]. British doctor Sir George Fredric Still called it an "abnormal defect of moral control" in children. That sounds pretty gruesome, but it was just an old-fashioned way of saying that some kids couldn't control their actions like others, despite being of normal intelligence.

It was then listed in the Diagnostic and Statistical Manual of Mental Disorders by the American Psychiatric Association in 1968, as a "hyperkinetic reaction of childhood". This appeared in the second edition of that hefty manual. But we're interested in the fifth edition, as that's where the current guidelines for a diagnosis of ADHD are found.

HOW ADHD IS DEFINED

Known as the DSM-5 Criteria[2], it covers these points.

1. Inattention in six or more of the following areas for kids aged 16 or under, or five or more for anyone older. These symptoms must have been notable for a minimum of six months.

    - Makes mistakes through carelessness or doesn't pay attention to details
    - Struggles to pay attention when working, studying, or playing
    - Doesn't seem to listen even when someone is speaking directly to them
    - Doesn't carry out instructions, meaning they get sidetracked and don't finish chores or tasks
    - Finds it difficult to organize the tasks they need to carry out

- They don't like things that involve a lot of mental effort for a period of time
- Regularly losing important things, like keys, books, phones
- Very easily distracted
- Forgetful even when carrying out normal, daily activities

2. Hyperactivity and impulsivity. Again, you're looking for six or more of these symptoms in someone 16 or younger, but only five for older people. And again, they need to have been present for at least six months.

- They have a habit of fidgeting, or they might tap their hands and feet or move around a lot when sitting
- Get up and move about when you'd expect them to stay seated
- Climbing and running around when they shouldn't. In the case of an adult, this might be limited to restlessness
- Doesn't seem able to play or take part in other leisure activities quietly
- Almost always on the go as though they've got a motor driving them
- Talks too much
- May quickly answer questions before they've been fully asked
- Finds it difficult to wait for their turn
- Interrupts other people when they're talking or by walking in on them

Other conditions are also listed in the diagnosis.

- Some of the above symptoms need to have been present before they reached the age of 12

- You should also see a number of these symptoms in more than one setting, so that could be at home and at work in adults, or at home and in school for children

- Another point that needs to be covered is that the symptoms reduce the quality of their social life or work

- It's also important to confirm that the symptoms can't be explained by other conditions or mental disorders, such as anxiety disorder or a mood disorder

I quickly counted enough symptoms in my ex to take this seriously. I read that the condition can look different in adults. Instead of running about and climbing trees, adults often wear out the people they're close to, for example. Speaking as a worn-out person, that struck a chord.

The list of symptoms in adults[3] continues with areas like disorganization, impulsiveness, poor time management, excessive activity, mood swings, poor planning ability, and problems dealing with stress.

THREE KINDS OF ADHD

Here are the three main kinds of ADHD that can be observed in different people.

1. Combined presentation is where the person has at least the stated minimum number of symptoms in both the inattention and hyperactivity-impulsivity sections

2. Predominantly inattentive presentation is where there are enough inattention symptoms but not enough hyperactivity-impulsivity in the last six months

3. Predominantly hyperactive-impulsive presentation is where there are sufficient hyperactivity-impulsivity symptoms but not the required amount of inattention.

Based on this information, you can see that not everyone with ADHD is going to act in the same way. The symptoms can change and adults who are aware of the issues may become adept at hiding the symptoms. Even from their partner.

But the big question is how can you tell if you are experiencing ADHD? Also, how can you tell if a partner is?

 In your Workbook you'll find a self-assessment quiz. You may choose to take it yourself or you may share it with your partner to get their involvement. Of course, some will complete the quiz on their partner's behalf.

I did something similar and became increasingly convinced that I'd found the answer to the questions I'd been asking. I'll point out here that diagnosing ADHD isn't like diagnosing the flu or a headache. This is a complex condition that varies from one person to another and can also change over time.

You may ask, but how did you *know*? After all, this is the most important point we've covered yet. Even medical experts struggle to get this diagnosis right.

HOW THE SYMPTOMS WORK IN REAL LIFE

I'll refer to my ex-partner as Sally. Sally and I were sitting in a restaurant once and I was complaining about my day at work. I admit that the story was not riveting. It was about how my boss had given me a job that I didn't want to do. The usual sort of thing that one might complain about with a partner then expect a nod and a pat on the arm in an attempt to sympathize. No big deal.

So there I was, moaning about meetings and conference calls and other things. And she was just ignoring me. She was sort of picking at the food without eating it. It was pasta with a fantastic sauce, by the way. I felt like such a fool as my epic complaint came to a stuttering end and Sally didn't say a word. That night, I couldn't get to sleep as I went over in my head what had happened. Had Sally ignored me because she thought I was being melodramatic? Had she fallen out of love with me?

On other occasions, different symptoms would emerge. I got an email saying that I'd been charged a small fortune because my bank account was in overdraft. I was furious because I knew it wasn't. I called the bank and after being tortured with hold music for the usual 20 minutes I vented my frustration at the poor woman on the phone.

"I know there's money in my account. My partner transferred money last week."

"One moment please."

Five minutes passed.

"When did you say your partner transferred the money?"

I put the phone on mute.

"Honey, what day did you make the transfer to my account?"

"Transfer? Was I meant to do that?"

This was when I started to get worried.

"Yeah, the transfer I asked you to do. To pay the rent ... last week."

Well, that's another symptom ticked off the list. And it wasn't the only time that her forgetfulness had caused us significant problems.

I don't want to give the impression that our life was a living hell. Most of the time it was great. The early love bubble effect may have worn off and we didn't swoon over each other all the time like before. But it still felt like a good, loving and healthy relationship. Most of the time.

Just the presence of ADHD in a relationship doesn't render it disastrous. In fact, it's rarely the ADHD that's the problem. It's usually the reaction of either or both partners to the circumstances caused by the presence of ADHD that destroys the relationship. This, of course, is exacerbated when either or both partners don't understand how ADHD operates. Worse still when there's not been a diagnosis.

Having something to attribute your partner's behavior to instead of putting it down to a lack of respect or love can be helpful. In fact, it can be enough to rescue a relationship that might otherwise be lost.

I found enough examples from my own experience to compile a small list of behaviors that are consistent with symptoms of ADHD. Perhaps these will help you to attribute behaviors you're witnessing to things other than a failing relationship.

As the partner of someone with ADHD you may feel that:

- You're ignored or lonely
- You do everything in the relationship
- Your partner doesn't value you highly enough
- You can't rely on or trust your partner
- You need to keep reminding them to do things
- You end up just doing things yourself

As the partner with ADHD you might feel that:

- You're constantly getting nagged or criticized
- Your partner is trying to control you all the time
- You need to constantly try and get your partner off your back
- Nothing you do ever seems to be good enough

We'll discuss these and other examples further. We'll also look at some case studies involving well-known people that have charted this course too. In these stories, you'll quickly discover that solutions do exist and they are accessible to you too.

THE MAIN CHALLENGES AND HOW TO FACE THEM TOGETHER

Knowing that a solution is available gives us energy to continue. With that, let's explore further into some of the challenges that partners can face when ADHD is also a part of the relationship.

1. Communication. The partners in this kind of relationship often seem to be in different worlds. You're worrying how to pay a bill and they're completely oblivious to it. Or you're trying to explain why you're feeling bad and they just seem to ignore you. This is where many of the problems come from, so it's the first area where we should be looking to improve. Talking to each other about this issue will help and we'll be looking at how to do that.

2. Time management and organization. In my case, this was probably the strongest cause of our problems. I hated seeing dirty dishes in the sink and dirty clothes in the laundry pile. It sounds silly but this kind of thing gets immensely annoying if you're like me. I ended up doing everything in the house and felt resentful about it. I'll admit that I accidentally smashed a couple of plates while washing them in a bad temper. Such was my frustration at the time!

3. Emotional regulation. Someone with ADHD may struggle to control their emotions. This can lead to them having outbursts that take their partner by surprise. We'll cover strategies for this because it's essential to separate behavior from reactions if a relationship is to last.

4. Being impulsive and hyperactive are two of the issues we think of as being part of this condition. Yet, we tend to think of kids jumping up and down or having tantrums. In adults, spending money impulsively and taking excessive risks are among the significant challenges. Living on instant noodles in the days before payday because your partner bought a tonne of lottery tickets isn't good for your long-term future together.

5. Intimacy. Of course, there are variations to this but in many cases ADHD will either rob you of your libido or fuel an insatiable sexual appetite. Understandably, this can create a chasm in even the most, otherwise, functional relationships.

Warning: Not everything you read about ADHD is true. Common misconceptions about ADHD lead to a thorough lack of understanding of the condition and, for our purposes, how it affects relationships. Just like the idea that every autistic person is a math genius, a series of ADHD myths exist. For example:

- Only boys can get it
- Only kids can get it
- It goes away on its own over time

- If someone isn't hyperactive they can't have ADHD
- It's a problem caused by bad parenting

Again, one of the biggest problems with this condition is that it's so badly misunderstood. Most people have a completely incorrect picture of it.

Why does this matter? The origins of the disease malaria can provide a clue. Malaria was common in marshy or swampy regions for centuries and killed millions of people across the planet. But everyone thought that it was caused by some sort of diseased air rising from the marshes. It's been suggested that the name comes from the Italian phrase for 'bad air' for this reason.

So, we couldn't treat malaria because we didn't understand what actually caused it. The real problem was only identified by scientists at the end of the 19th century. The real culprits – mosquitoes – would have gotten away with it if it wasn't for the persistent puzzling of those scientists.

Myths are not always helpful. Particularly where they relate to anything of importance.

This book is designed to clear up the issues that stop people from recognizing ADHD and doing something about it. That includes destroying some outdated myths that could be getting in the way of your loving, healthy, respectful relationships.

Like any problem in life, the first step is to clearly identify it. If you've got a sore tooth you don't just pull it out without first going to a dentist to find out what's wrong. So, let's go back to the beginning and imagine a couple struggling because of some of the issues we've explored here.

A man is acting irresponsibly. He forgets about his relationship anniversary and, that day, arrives home late. His partner complains about his attitude but he's not even listening. The next day something triggers his memory about the anniversary and he impulsively spends more than he can afford on an over-the-top gift for his partner. Now he's in debt and she's got a day-late gift she didn't even want.

What does his partner think of all this? Maybe she thinks he's having an affair and suddenly felt guilty about it. Or perhaps she thinks he's bored with their relationship and is plucking up the courage to tell her. Their communication may become strained or even non-existent for a couple of days.

It's only by understanding her partner's condition that she can understand her partner better. This doesn't mean that his behavior is fine. But at least their attempts to resolve things are focused on the cause rather than blaming "bad air" while being bitten alive by mosquitos!

DISPELING THE ADHD MYTHS YOU'VE HEARD

Now, as for those unhelpful myths we listed earlier, here are the reasons why they're neither helpful nor real:

- Only boys can get it. Just not true, The Centers for Disease Control reports that boys are three times more likely[4] to be diagnosed with ADHD. That doesn't necessarily mean that they're more affected, though. The issue here is that it's more difficult to detect in girls because the symptoms are generally more subtle.

- Only kids can get it. Again, not true[5]. It is true that more kids are diagnosed with it, but there are some possible reasons for this. For example, parents are more likely to recognize some symptoms and therefore get a diagnosis than, say, an adult partner is, based on their observations of their partner's behavior.

- It goes away on its own over time. Sometimes this can happen, but this is not a reliable outcome. This belief is probably linked to the fact that people think only kids get it, so it must somehow disappear as they grow up, right? But that doesn't happen in every case[6].

- If someone isn't hyperactive they can't have ADHD. Being hyperactive is one of the symptoms but we've seen that it isn't the only sign to look out for. It's perfectly possible to have ADHD and not display hyperactivity.

- It's a problem caused by bad parenting. Or bad partners! Let's move away from blaming others. It makes no sense and can make it more difficult to get help. ADHD is a neurodevelopmental issue that we don't yet fully understand[7]. Possible causes include genetics, brain injuries, and environmental factors.

We'll also be looking at all the challenges and solutions from every angle. Maybe you're in exactly the same situation I was in. Or perhaps you're the partner with ADHD and you've taken this step of finding out more on your own. Or you both have ADHD.

Understanding and supporting your loved one is vital in any of these situations. It's a challenge you need to rise to, but this is easier said than done. It's far from impossible, though.

This is only going to work if you genuinely feel the need to make it work. You're only going to make such an effort for a relationship that you're prepared to work for.

You're going to need a lot of determination and patience. But that's not all. Great communication is needed to avoid your good intentions coming up short. In fact, this has probably been one of the major issues that have caused you to start this book. You're looking for help to communicate better even if you didn't know that at the beginning.

What this isn't about is blaming and shaming. It's about finding a way to work through this issue together. Because that's how you're going to get through it. Together.

You've made a great start by getting this book and reading through the first chapter. That means you're now on your way to understanding what to do. But let's not get ahead of ourselves because there's still a lot to cover here.

You can't understand this purely through luck. You need to work at it and learn everything you need to know. Education and understanding are the key concepts here. The more you know about ADHD and coping strategies, the better your chances of getting your relationship on track.

So. we'll call this the first step successfully completed.

You now know the basics, and upon that, you can build a greater understanding.

More importantly, you know that strong relationships are still possible.

This takes me back to my own situation. Now is a good moment to reveal that we finally got back together. How did we do it? To find out, you'll need to venture into the following chapters. This is where we'll start to look more deeply at the challenges ahead. We'll be looking at strategies I've used successfully. I know they work and I can show you how to adapt them to your unique life and circumstances.

Are you ready? I'm waiting for you in Chapter 2 where your journey towards a successful relationship continues …

2

COMMON CHALLENGES AND PROVEN COPING STRATEGIES

The Things We All Go Through

The key to life is accepting challenges. Once someone stops doing this, he's dead.

— Bette Davis

You now know the ADHD symptoms and you've probably identified them in some real-life situations just like I did. But you're still not convinced that something positive can be done. Is this simply something you need to live with? Thankfully, it isn't.

The next step is to fully understand the symptoms and how to manage them. We need to look at different scenarios that might seem familiar to you. Then we need coping strategies for each situation. They aren't definitive solutions. Rather, these are tips that will help you deal with the ups and downs. A starting point for getting life together back on track.

If you do this well, you're well on the road to a better relationship and life.

Let's start by going back to some of the specific symptoms we looked at in the last chapter, and fill in more details. Then we can look at how to cope. You'll see that the same coping strategies crop up for different situations, and that's fine. It's all about finding the right mix of strategies for your own, unique situation.

 The problem - You're ignored or lonely

The symptoms - So you might be telling them about your day or what needs to be done in the house and they seem to be a million miles away. Getting angry doesn't help. Shouting doesn't help. Sometimes you just feel so *helpless*.

 The coping strategy - One useful tip here is that a lot of people with ADHD function better with a clear routine. Maybe you could set aside a certain time of day to discuss important matters. Is your partner usually more attentive and concentrated in the

Common ChallengeS and Proven Coping Strategies

morning or in the evening, for example? Talk to your partner when they're most likely to listen and interact. It's going to take patience, so choose those times when *you're* feeling positive and ready to give it your best shot too.

The problem - You do everything in the relationship

The symptoms - You just end up doing everything because your partner forgets to do it or loses concentration. Cleaning, washing the dishes, cooking, and paying bills. It's all part of your life now, but no one can carry on doing all this forever unless they're some sort of domestic servant robot and I'm guessing you're not made of metal and circuit boards. So, you're exhausted and feeling under-appreciated right now.

The coping strategy - You need to get your partner to focus on their tasks. One way some people do this is through the use of reminders. Sticky notes, smartphone alarms, and a kitchen board with notes can all help. Of course, the risk is that they feel nagged, so get their agreement to approach it in this way before expecting them to suddenly be on board.

The problem - Your partner doesn't value you highly enough

The symptoms - In this case, the symptoms are actually related to the other areas we've looked at, aren't they? It's not that your partner doesn't value you. The problem is that they're struggling with ADHD. So if we can solve the other areas we're looking at, this point should be covered too.

The coping strategy - The changes need to happen inside your head. Use the information you're learning here to turn this point

31

around. It's not that your partner doesn't value you. They simply need your help to make the relationship a functional two-way exchange. Look at life from their point of view to understand their challenges.

 The problem - *You can't rely on or trust your partner*

The symptoms - They let you down time and time again. You're left waiting out in the rain or they forget to buy something you need. It's like having a child rather than an adult partner sometimes, and you don't want all this hassle.

 The coping strategy - Help them get organized with reminders and alarms. Communication is hugely important. Don't treat your partner like a child or as an incompetent person. Routines are fantastic in this situation. They help you to keep life on an even keel and soon become second nature.

 The problem - *You need to keep reminding them to do things / You end up just doing things yourself*

The symptoms - We're starting to see that a lot of these problems tie in together. There's a crossover between symptoms and the lines get blurred. You feel like your life is going around in ever-decreasing circles. Nothing ever gets done unless you do it yourself. You're getting burnt out without ever getting anywhere.

 The coping strategy - Help the other person to deal with their ADHD. Be understanding and kind but doing everything for them is just delaying the inevitable moment when you explode because it's all too much for you. From personal experience, I'd also suggest 'loosening up a bit'. You might not find that in any

Common Challenges and Proven Coping Strategies

medical textbooks but I made the conscious decision to not get so uptight about anything that didn't really matter.

The points we've looked at above relate to people in the situation I was in with Sally. I know how frustrating they are, but looking at those coping strategies helps us see the way forward with more clarity. Carry out a few steps and we can begin to feel in control of life again.

It's a long process but once you've taken your first steps you'll see the mist lift and the road ahead will look a lot clearer.

But what about people in Sally's situation? I asked what she felt as our relationship spun out of control and almost crash-landed. At first, she didn't want to talk about it, and I realized that she'd been more deeply hurt by these problems than I'd imagined.

I had thought that I was the victim and that she was somehow oblivious to the problems. This wasn't true, of course. Yet, she eventually told me how bad she'd felt in the following ways.

The problem - *You're constantly getting nagged or criticized*

The symptoms - Being nagged and criticized, I guess. As the person who was nagging and criticizing, I can confirm that I was exceptionally good at it and harassed her wonderfully well. Sally told me that she felt like a naughty child again, being told off for every little thing. She already felt terrible about the things she forgot but me nagging her about them made everything much worse.

The coping strategy. I asked Sally how we should have coped and she said with better communication. Honestly, if I'd known how

33

much my nagging affected her I would have looked for solutions a lot earlier, but our communication had totally broken down. It doesn't matter who opens up the communication channels as long as one of you does. If you do it today then so much the better.

 The problem - Your partner is trying to control you all the time

The symptoms - You feel as though you can't be trusted to do anything. Your partner clearly thinks that you are useless and that affects your self-esteem and confidence.

 The coping strategy - Sally tells me that I should have let her make her own mistakes. That's easier said than done but I can see her point. I was running about like crazy vacuuming up all her oversights and constantly fire-fighting on her behalf. She admits she should have told me to stop, but I honestly don't know if I would have accepted that advice.

 The problem - You need to constantly try and get your partner off your back

The symptoms - Yes, I was the awful partner who watched Sally over her shoulder as she wrote messages and double-checked the bank account every time she said she'd done something. I was like some sort of daily reminder that she couldn't be trusted to do things.

 The coping strategy - The partner with ADHD could cope by sending messages to the other partner to let them know they've completed something important. Such as paying a bill. Just a short message, maybe make it into something funny. Of course, it needs to be a two-way street, so I now send messages to Sally when I need to let her know I've done something that affects both of us. All part of the communication strategy you need.

The problem - *Nothing you do ever seems to be good enough*

The symptoms - This is the one that really hit me hard. All this time I'd been giving out the impression that Sally was useless. No matter how hard she tried - and she was trying - I sent back the message that she wasn't trying hard enough.

The coping strategy - Both partners should take advantage of the good times and the relaxed moments. Let the special person in your life know that you appreciate most of what they do. There's just this one area that's hurting you, so don't make it into what defines your relationship.

OTHER STRATEGIES TO BEAR IN MIND

I'm sure those coping strategies will help you. They cover the main points that I've found useful, but there are other strategies and techniques I'd like to share with you.

Yoga, mindfulness meditation, and other stress-reduction techniques are vital. My stress levels were through the roof and these things really helped me. Personally, I would put on some relaxing music like natural rainforest sounds and try out a few yoga positions. It felt fantastic and soon became my refuge.

It's up to you what you focus your mind on while meditating. You could think about solutions to your current problems, solve world hunger, or let yourself drift away. Trying to meditate with a blank mind is a lot more difficult for me but it might feel right for some people.

Getting enough exercise is also important, as this boosts your endorphins and protects you from the harmful effects of stress[8]. I went walking a lot as I live near some quiet country lanes where I could go out and just have some cows and donkeys for company.

Sleep is crucial too. Don't let anyone tell you that sleep doesn't matter. If you're not getting enough hours of shut-eye[9] then your mental state and decision-making are going to go haywire. Meditating and exercising in the evening can help. I also like to write down a list of things to do the next day, as that helps me to clear my mind at the end of the day.

MEDICATION OPTIONS

You'll need to know about the different types of ADHD medication currently available as well. Not everyone is comfortable with the idea of taking medication while others perhaps throw themselves into this too enthusiastically.

I would say that medication could be helpful but isn't the only solution. You can't just take medication and expect the problems to disappear. Having said that, it makes sense to check out what's available to you. The following are the most important areas.

Stimulants

The first category is stimulants and this is the most popular kind of medication for ADHD, working for a majority of people according to online sources[24]. They help you to focus and stop distractions from getting in the way by boosting your dopamine and norepinephrine levels and getting nerves in the brain to communicate better. Depending upon where you live, you might get offered the likes of Amphetamine/dextroamphetamine (Adderall), Dexmethylphenidate (Focalin), or Amphetamine sulfate (Evekeo) among others. You don't need to memorize those names but check online when a specific medicine is offered to you. You can then check that it's a safe, recommended medicine.

Non-stimulants

This option is often offered to those people who don't see any positive changes from stimulants, or suffer nasty side effects from them. Unlike stimulants, they're not classed as controlled substances in most countries. They work in one of two ways, with Atomoxetine (Strattera) being the most common example of a norepinephrine modulator. Clonidine (Catapres, Kapvay) is an example from the alpha agonists category. Again, no need to memorize these names. Just refer to reliable sources when a medication is suggested to you and you want to make sure that you know what it is.

Antidepressants

This is another option but rather than replacing the stimulants or non-stimulants, antidepressants are most commonly used together with them. This can be an alternative way of helping you by boosting the amount of dopamine (a feel-good chemical) and norepinephrine (which is a neurotransmitter that determines your fight-or-flight response) in your brain. Some of the common antidepressants you might come across for ADHD include Bupropion (Wellbutrin) and Venlafaxine (Effexor).

With all of these types of medication, it's important that you seek professional medical advice and then follow it. Don't just start taking pills. You need to know what you've been given and why. No one expects you to become a pharmaceutical expert, but you need to understand the reasons behind using a certain pill and how it's meant to work.

THE THERAPY OPTION

Getting therapy for ADHD is a valid option and definitely worth considering. You'll generally see it split into the following types.

Cognitive-behavioral therapy (CBT) for ADHD[10]

This is a fairly short-term type of psychotherapy that's designed to help change how you feel about yourself. Ideally, it gives you a way to change your internal dialog and remove the damaging thought patterns caused by ADHD. Someone who has become highly self-critical and formed a pessimistic view of themselves could find therapy hugely helpful.

Couples therapy

Going to therapy sessions with your partner can be a fantastic way of showing that you're in this together. This is a way to look at the issues in your relationship and understand them better. I went to several sessions with Sally and it was difficult at first but it's definitely a way to get the difficult conversations started in a controlled environment.

Family therapy

This is similar to couples therapy but tends to be used mainly in the cases of children with ADHD. I would suggest not getting too hung up on the name of the therapy. Sitting down with a professional and opening up on your deepest fears and biggest hopes is worthwhile no matter what it's called.

ALTERNATIVE TREATMENTS

I've always liked looking for alternatives, which explains why I gargle salt water and drink ginger tea whenever I feel under the weather. If only dealing with ADHD was as simple as this.

The treatments we've looked at already are all recommended and I wouldn't suggest using the following ideas instead of them.

Having said that, these alternative treatments are excellent if used in addition to the other methods. These are changes to your life that you can make right away and feel almost instant benefits. Take a look to see which ones you might be interested in trying.

- Nutritional and dietary interventions. I'm always amazed at people who say that their life improves just by eliminating a certain food. It's not really something we tried and there's no official ADHD diet, but the best dietary advice for ADHD is just to eat fresh and healthy. Cut out highly processed and refined sugar as an immediate start.

- Supplements. There's a lot of advice out there about different supplements for ADHD [11], like zinc, iron, and vitamin D. A study on children[12] suggests that changing the omega-3 / omega-6 balance in our bodies might be useful, but it's not conclusive.

- Exercise and physical activity. This is one activity that I can heartily recommend to everyone whether they've got ADHD or not. We started taking long walks together to talk about life. I can't be completely sure if it was the walking or the talking that helped but it was probably a combination of the two. Find an exercise you can do together, like cycling or golf, if possible.

- Mind-body interventions. This is another area I'm going to strongly recommend. I tried yoga alone and it really helped me to feel calmer. Sally then joined me and we had some relaxing times together just stretching and feeling at peace with the world.

- Alternative therapies such as acupuncture and massage. These are a couple of other therapies we're thinking of trying soon. Acupuncture is used by many people to treat ADHD and there are reasons to believe that it could work[13]. But more studies are needed.

The final point I want to leave you with is that there's no single cure. There's no miracle. Just coping strategies and your willpower.

I suggest trying as many of the alternative methods as you can safely manage. Supplements are the one area to be extra careful around, while everything else is just good advice for a healthy body and mind.

Combine the alternative methods you most like with the medicine and other treatments given to you by a medical expert. It's then a question of sustaining it.

Don't make it boring. This isn't a chore just to get over with. Neither is this an endurance test designed to push you to the limits of human suffering.

It's a chance to improve your life together and most of the ideas we've looked at are pretty good fun. We vary our routine by walking one day, doing yoga the next, and trying different healthy recipes.

You can see by now why we can't even say with certainty what exactly helped Sally control her ADHD symptoms. She didn't take a pill and then suddenly feel better. There was no eureka moment. This was a gradual process and I'm so grateful that we went through it together.

I have to admit that I feel healthier and in a better frame of mind thanks to those strategies. That was a benefit I hadn't expected, but doing those activities together was great for *my* mind and body as well as Sally's.

If I had my time over again, I know I could fast-track the process of getting to a healthier, happier place together. If I knew then what I know now, I would have built at least a rough plan showing how we would experiment with all the available options. We would have applied them, tested them and known what was working. It would have been more systematic and effective than our trial-and-error approach. We got there but we could have done it better.

With this in mind, I've created an exercise in the Workbook that will allow you to make the plan that I would like to have made. You'll see all the options laid out for you and space for you to create your plan. It will save you weeks, if not months of guesswork.

In addition to our experimenting and trial-and-error, we know without any doubt that communication was the key to getting on the right path. Now is a good time to see how we learned to get past our communication frustrations. That's a heck of a story in its own right so strap yourself in for an interesting ride.

3

WAIT. WHAT WAS I SAYING?

How To Establish Effective Communication Between You

I think for any relationship to be successful, there needs to be loving communication, appreciation, and understanding.

– Miranda Kerr

A lot of what we've touched on so far is about communication. It's already clear that this is one of the keys to getting an ADHD relationship on track. If your communication is poor, the issues coming from ADHD will only get worse.

Let's start by seeing why this matters so much. What are the specific communication challenges caused by ADHD? Is there no way to get by without resolving this?

One of the main problems with ADHD is that it can be difficult for the person affected to pay attention and listen. They struggle to stay focused. This makes effective communication incredibly difficult, leading to frustration and a further breakdown in communication.

You probably already know that communication is incredibly important in every relationship. This is how you:

- Get to know each other
- Build trust
- Avoid any misunderstandings
- Clear up problems
- Set your expectation levels for one another

If any of those communication benefits are missing, your relationship is going to be strained. Imagine your partner spoke a different language to yours and you couldn't understand a single word each other said. No matter how much you liked the idea of being with them, a meaningful relationship would be impossible until you found a way to speak each other's language.

Maybe we can look at ADHD like that. You are like two people who speak different languages. What you need is to find common ground. You need to be able to communicate effectively. Without that starting point, you're going nowhere.

Thankfully, it's not going to be as difficult as learning the grammatical rules of a new language. But you're going to have to learn how to communicate in a way that gets through to each other.

What are some of the problems that your partner might be having right now? The following are common issues for people with ADHD.

- They're easily distracted. This is a conversation-killer, as you're talking and notice that they're looking at their phone or doing something else. You think it's because they find you boring or maybe they're thinking about someone else. You can see how misunderstandings begin so easily.

- It can be difficult to organize their thoughts. Let's say that your partner wants to discuss the future with you but can't work out exactly what to say. So they say nothing. And you see that as a sign that they're not interested in a future together.

- They can't get their ideas across well. Again, the problem here is that you're not seeing what they really think. They might be extremely excited about making plans with you but are unable to explain that well. So you're unable to understand what they really think.

- They might miss something important you've said. We all hate it when someone doesn't listen to us. It's even worse when it's your partner. If you realize that they haven't listened and missed something you said, the normal reaction is to get frustrated. It can also lead to practical issues such as not paying bills on time or not meeting when you're meant to.

- They're impulsive and interrupt you. Every couple wants free-flowing conversations that go back and forward. If one of you interrupts the other too much, it's going to stop you in your tracks. That frustration level is going to go through the roof too.

Good communication with your partner has to be the basic building block of your relationship. What will happen if you stay together for 10 or 15 years, or longer? Without good communication, all of these issues will just get bigger and bigger. You'll feel trapped in a world where no one listens and you can't get to know each other on a deeper level.

Misunderstanding and misinterpretations are common in relationships with ADHD. You both *think* you know what the other one means or is going to do. But the truth is that you're just guessing a lot of the time.

You mentioned paying the bills earlier and she kind of nodded before talking about something else. So now, you're left wondering if it was a yes or no. Did she even hear you? It's easy to see how you could end up assuming a lot of the time and being wrong often.

We're back at frustration again, aren't we? Even a simple matter like arranging when to meet or working out who is going to wash the dishes can turn into a major challenge.

What makes this worse is that someone with ADHD may have trouble reading social cues. Interpreting nonverbal communication can be a problem too. Knowing this, you can easily see why you might feel misunderstood or unheard.

No relationship can thrive in this sort of situation. We've seen how important communication is in a relationship. Now we need to look at the opposite of the benefits of good communication that we saw earlier. A lack of communication leads to:

- Not being able to get to know each other deeply
- A lack of trust
- Regular misunderstandings
- Problems just keep growing and getting worse
- You aren't clear on what to expect from one another

All of this leads to you feeling unsatisfied. You're not getting everything that you need from this relationship. You feel that you deserve more. You deserve a partner who listens to you. You deserve the chance to build a strong, loving relationship.

The relationship is going to suffer. You're going to feel that they're not taking you into account. They're not looking at things from your perspective. You try to point this out but it doesn't help. Trying to improve a relationship with non-existent communication is incredibly difficult.

So you get frustrated. And you get angry. You're feeling isolated and alone. I know because I've been there.

What about the person on the other side, though? What are they feeling? After talking to Sally, it seems that we both felt similarly. She was frustrated and angry and isolated too. So we were both suffering at the same time. Imagine the difference if we could have communicated with each other.

It was like I was slowly sinking. Instead of being my liferaft, Sally was drowning alongside me. And neither of us knew how to help the other. We both wanted the same outcome but neither of us knew what to do.

STRATEGIES FOR EFFECTIVE COMMUNICATION

The good news is that it's possible to stay afloat. The following are the strategies for effective communication that I recommend.

Active Listening

This may sound complicated but it's really not. Active listening is vital for couples dealing with ADHD. It's about paying close attention when other people speak. You need to reflect back what you've heard. Asking for confirmation that you've understood correctly is helpful. You can also ask questions to clarify your understanding.

To carry out active listening well, you should summarize or paraphrase what you've heard. You might say, "So, you've ordered the food and now you want me to pick up the drinks?" or "9 o'clock is fine then, but if I get there earlier there's no problem?"

You're not putting the other person under pressure or making them feel nervous. Those examples above shouldn't be said as "You've got the food, right? I'm only getting the drinks, so I'm counting on you to not forget the food" or "Are you sure you'll be there at 9? Because the last time you said that…"

Open-ended questions are necessary too. These are great for getting the other person in the conversation to open up and communicate more easily.

Open-ended questions can be formulated by starting with words like how or why, or you could start the question with 'tell me about…' or 'what do you think…'. In this way, you're encouraging them to open up more. This is a great starting point but that's all it is.

To keep the conversation flowing, you need to give their answer your full attention. This is why it's important to start when there are no distractions and you can both concentrate on the conversation.

Let's look at a couple of examples of active and passive listening.

Active Listening Example

We can start with what not to do.

You: You forgot to collect the car from the garage again, didn't you? I had to leave work early to go and get it.

Your Partner: Did I?

You: Yes, you did. Did you not stop to think that I might be busy too? Why didn't you just let me know or tell me you were busy because I was busy too and you didn't think of that, did you?

Although you're asking several questions, they are all rhetorical. At no point are you encouraging them to take part in the conversation. You're not looking for their opinion or giving them the chance to contribute by explaining why they didn't do what they were meant to do.

Now let's take a look at how this conversation could have been carried out better using active listening and open-ended questions.

You: What happened that made you forget to go to the garage today?

Your Partner: Was that today? I thought it was tomorrow.

You: I had to leave work early. What do you think we should do to stop the same thing happening again the next time?

Your Partner: I don't know.

You: Tell me what kind of reminder might help you.

Your Partner: Maybe something in the calendar on my phone.

You: How would you feel if I let you know when an appointment like this is due?

Of course, in the second example you're just as frustrated and annoyed as in the first example. But the difference is that you're being smarter about looking for solutions. You're doing this by letting your partner get involved and feel that they're contributing. You're not just throwing all the blame at them without looking for their thoughts on the matter.

The Use Of Validation And Empathy

This is a concept that we're going to be going back to a lot during the rest of the book. These are crucial ideas in building trust and creating a stronger connection. In relationships that are affected by ADHD, this becomes an even more important matter.

What is validation? This is where you acknowledge that the other person has their own point of view. You're accepting that their feelings are valid, even if you don't agree with them. This is crucial because you're saying that what they feel matters. You're not automatically jumping in and saying that they're wrong. Instead, you're giving them a chance to express their feelings and you're accepting them without judgment or criticism.

Does it matter who's right and who's wrong? There are obviously situations in which this is the case and you need to know which opinion is correct. You don't want to make bad financial decisions or make mistakes in other important areas of life. But there are plenty of other, more minor areas of daily life too. Using validation means that you're agreeing that your relationship is a two-way street rather than just a question of being right or wrong.

What is empathy? We hear this word used a lot but do you really know what it means? Empathy is described as being the ability to understand someone else's feelings or situation. It's about walking a mile in someone else's shoes.

Being empathetic comes naturally to some people but not to everyone. Thankfully, you can learn this skill even if it isn't natural for you. Learn to look at life through your partner's eyes and you'll gain a valuable new perspective.

You'll understand that there's always a reason for what they do and what they don't do. Don't jump in and judge them right away. The first step is always to take a moment and consider what might have happened.

Going back to the example of picking up a car from the garage, your first instinct might be to get angry. But what if your partner genuinely forgot or got distracted? What if they had every intention of doing this all morning but didn't carry it through? They probably feel terrible about it now, right? Imagine how you would feel if you let important details like this slip through your fingers. Having someone who understands and doesn't judge you would be a massive help.

The use of validation and empathy helps to reduce conflict in any relationship. You're showing that the other person matters and that their point of view matters. Don't you think that should be the starting point for any sort of serious relationship?

The Power Of "I" Statements

You might have been told at some point that it's not polite to talk a lot about yourself. We're often advised that it's better to talk about other people and not ourselves. While this is good advice in general, there are certain situations where using "I" statements makes a lot of sense.

This is a way of letting the other person know how you feel without blaming them or firing off accusations. It's a smart way of focusing the conversation on your feelings and point of view. So you're shifting away from assuming what the other person feels or how they acted.

A few examples of how you can turn an accusing phrase into something more constructive will help us get a feel for this.

1. "You made me go and collect the car from the garage" becomes "I didn't feel very comfortable leaving my job early to get the car."
2. "It was so thoughtless of you to leave me standing out there in the rain" becomes "I felt silly standing there all wet and not knowing what to do."
3. "You forgot to pay the bills again this month" becomes "I'm worried about how we can make sure we pay the bills on time in the future.
4. "You never listen to me" becomes "I feel frustrated when I can't get my point across to you effectively."

Can you see how the focus is changed in these alternative statements? We're taking some of the pressure off our partners by not putting them immediately on the defensive.

Nonviolent Communication

Respect has to be at the heart of your relationship. The fact that you're wrestling with the presence of ADHD is no excuse for losing the respect and trust that needs to exist. This leads us to nonviolent communication. Another way of looking at this is how we can cut out the risk of our frustrations escalating into physical violence or overly harsh words.

There's no secret to nonviolent communication. If you've put into action the areas we've already at, this is the next logical step.

Your main responsibility is to find a way to express your feelings and what you need respectfully. You need to be clear and direct, but if there's one word I don't want you to forget it's respect.

Four steps are needed here and they are as follows:

1. Observation. You're not evaluating or putting your own spin on events. All you're doing is observing and putting what you observe into context.

2. Feelings. This is where you add your own feelings or thoughts. However, the approach is to keep them separate from other thoughts. By identifying whether your needs are being met and opening up to vulnerability, you should be able to connect more easily with your partner.

3. Needs. The Center for Nonviolent Communication has created a needs inventory[14] that lets us see what basic, universal human needs we all need to be met. Amongst others, they include: connection, physical wellbeing, honesty, play, peace, autonomy, and meaning. Knowing this allows to understand what is driving the actions of others and to communicate our needs in terms that others understand.

4. Requests. You want to clearly request what you feel you need. But it's not a demand. If your partner says no then your task is to empathize with what is stopping them from agreeing with you.

Taking all four steps into account, we can see the full process needed. You observe the situation, Then you identify your feelings about it. You work out which of your basic needs are causing the feelings. Finally, you clearly request an action that would address that need. The steps above are repeated in your Workbook with an exercise that relates to your own relationship scenarios.

It might all sound too simple to be true. But nonviolent communication can be highly effective at lowering the risk of conflict in an ADHD relationship. At the very least, it can diffuse a situation before feelings get hurt and damage is done to the trust that is vital to the health of your relationship.

The Benefits Of Creating A Communication Plan

Setting some communication goals can be useful. These can be simple statements like not going to bed angry and not letting a day pass without speaking about the relationship. They let you both know that you're on the same page and working out how to make the relationship better.

It's also worth programming catch-up days. Maybe you're both free on Sunday mornings or Saturday evenings. If so, make that the time when you go to the park together or sit in the garden or whatever helps you to unwind and connect.

Don't forget to use technology to do what it does best. It can be a great way to stay connected even when you're far apart. Just sending short messages a few times a day is a fantastic way to let your partner know that they're in your thoughts.

Communication During Conflict

Communication is a lot easier during simple times when everything is going well. It's more of a challenge during times of conflict, though. This is when you need to go back to the basic principles that we've looked at.

Empathy and validation are especially important during conflicts. You can use these techniques to de-escalate conflicts. Also, remember to use the nonviolent communication steps we've looked at.

Having said that, this is also a good moment to introduce some new principles. The more de-escalation techniques you have the better, so let's add the following to the list of tools you've got available to you.

- Identifying triggers and how to avoid them. Are there certain "touchy" subjects that you need to stay away from?

- Rejection, betrayal, and feeling helpless are some of the most common. Take the time to understand you and your partner's triggers.

- How to control your emotions when a trigger is hit. Think about the way you react to any of those touchy subjects. Can you do something to regulate your emotions? Start by identifying them[15,] with the biggest signs generally including a thumping heart, dizziness, or sweating palms. You can then look for advice on how to control those specific symptoms using techniques like breathing deeply and cutting off negative thoughts.

- Take a time-out. Sometimes, the best approach is to walk away and cool off. We can all get caught up in the moment, but taking a step back can help you to see the situation more clearly and start again.

- Think about going back to it later. This point isn't about ignoring the issue and hoping that it goes away. Instead, you're admitting that now isn't the right time to resolve it. You might decide to set aside time later to revisit it and see if you can find the perfect solution then.

We All Have Different Styles

Have you ever thought about your partner's communication style? We all have one so if you haven't yet identified it you need to know. You also need to know your own communication style, These basic styles will help to identify your respective communication styles[16]. There is space dedicated to this process in your Workbook.

- Passive communication is carried out when you don't express your feelings or needs. You let other people make decisions to avoid conflict, but that may lead to resentment building up. Example: "We'll just do whatever you think is best"

- Aggressive communication is where the person expresses their own feelings but doesn't respect others'. They may be hostile or go on the defensive, and they often hurt others with this approach. Example: "You need to do as I say".

- Passive-aggressive communication is where you seem passive and accepting but anger may be simmering under the surface. Example: sarcastic answers and avoiding the subject

- Assertive communication is where you communicate directly and honestly while respecting others. Example: "I need us to find a way to solve this issue today".

Each of those approaches has good and bad points you need to be aware of, and some of them combine better than others in a relationship.

You need to look at strategies for bridging the communication gaps and working together to find a way of communicating effectively. This means avoiding making assumptions, keeping the message clear, and checking your partner's comprehension. Again, in your Workbook, you will find space to work on this.

Learn More, Love More (About ADHD)

You both need to know as much as possible about ADHD. This will help you both understand how it affects you and the relationship. This can be done in several ways, but remember to try and keep it interesting.

You've already seen that reading books about ADHD is a fantastic idea. You're going to learn even more as you progress in this book.

There are documentaries and movies to watch together as well. Free The Mind and The Disruptors are a couple of names to bear in mind. You'll also want to keep an eye out for any TV shows coming up on this subject, as they often cover this condition in interesting ways with real-life examples.

Did you know that celebrities like Paris Hilton, Solange Knowles, and Michelle Rodriguez have all experienced ADHD[17]? Following their stories can be an entertaining way of learning more about this subject without it seeming too heavy. Autobiographies such as Chasing Kites: A Memoir About Growing Up With ADHD by Tom Nardone give you another alternative.

Multiple Olympic gold winner Simone Biles was revealed to be ADHD when details of her mediation were leaked. She then told the world it was nothing to be ashamed about. Another Olympian hero. Michael Phelps, credits swimming with helping him keep his ADHD symptoms under control. There are plenty of other stories about famous people that could inspire you and teach you at the same time.

Basically, there are many different ways of finding out more about how to deal with this struggle. But nothing beats talking to one another. All of those ideas - and this book - are designed to be ways to get the conversation started.

Find a way to communicate and to understand each other and this will lead you to better times with a deeper sense of connection and love.

How exactly will you do this? I think every couple has to find their own way of doing it that suits them, but here are some ideas you can use.

- Share the responsibilities. This is a condition that affects both of you and you need to work together to make it a less important negative factor in your relationship. You both need to "own" this condition, rather than it being all put onto the shoulders of the person who suffers the symptoms.

- Set your expectation levels. We've already seen how crucial it is to communicate your expectations, and this is something that gets you started with a clear sense of a shared goal

- No more blame. This is no one's fault and that means neither of you has to shoulder any guilty feelings about the problems you go through.

- Set aside time. Finding out more about how ADHD affects both of you is only going to happen with time and patience. This is a long-term project and it's worth the time and effort you're planning to put into it.

Don't be put off by the thought that this is going to be difficult. Your communication strategy is at the heart of your plan to stop ADHD from being a problem that keeps you from enjoying a loving relationship.

Your Workbook is a great resource for this where you can work on your communication strategy and build a plan that will help you navigate to much better outcomes through more effective communication. You may like to use the LearnWell Community to find and share ideas.

How will you find the time to implement your new communication strategy? I realize that timekeeping is one of the major issues with couples fighting against ADHD; so the next chapter is going to tell you how to deal with this. You'll also find out about some of the mistakes we made that left us standing outside a locked door feeling helpless.

4

WHERE DID THE TIME GO? AND WHERE ARE MY KEYS?

Managing Time And Being (More) Organized

Time is really the only capital that any human being has, and the only thing he can't afford to lose.

– Thomas Edison

The hands of time are always spinning around, forcing us to try and keep up. Modern life is all about rushing and being constantly occupied. So who's got the time to deal with the extra issues caused by ADHD? The truth is that lost time is probably the biggest cost to your relationship.

When I think about lost time I remember how we canceled trips and evenings out because of a lack of organization. Lost keys, lost tickets, and lost directions ended up souring anything we wanted to do away from home.

So it's easier to stay at home. But then time just slips away one minute at a time as you regret not doing *something special*.

I remember the frustration of sitting and watching a reality show that I hated because we had to cancel a trip to the coast. We had rushed out and closed the front door behind us. And the keys?

Dangling from the door. On the inside.

It was a horrible sinking feeling, We were locked out and panicking.

We eventually got it opened, but we'd been running behind time anyway. And now the train was long gone, already winding along the route to the coast without us. So it was another Saturday spent at home.

Of course, spending quality time with your partner should be fun wherever you are. But if you've got a sense of frustration and missed opportunities bubbling away inside you, it's not going to be such quality time, is it?

Let's go back to the beginning of that story about the keys. I'm not going to tell you what we should have done differently, because that's obvious. Instead, let's look at how we handled it. What can we learn from the mistakes made?

As the door slammed shut, it was Sally who turned to me and uttered those fateful words, "The keys...". She'd realized before I did that they were inside the door. The color drained from my face and I felt my legs go weak.

At this point, you might ask whose fault it was. Did one of us have the specific job of taking the keys out of the door? Whose keys were they anyway? Who closed the door without looking? Was there even a key holder in this relationship?

AVOID FALLING INTO THE BLAME GAME TRAP

I think most of us naturally fall into the trap of carrying out the blame game. Possibly because we feel silly when something goes wrong. I know I felt stupid about closing the door with the keys still stuck in it. So my first reaction was to blame Sally. After all, they were her keys. Weren't they?

Ah, she replied, so where are your keys? I told her she'd lost them last month and had forgotten to get another set cut. So she told me that I had been using her keys since then. Technically those were *my* keys in the door.

Can you see how pointless it is to blame one another? We just went around in circles for a few minutes, trying to find the perfect piece of evidence to pin the blame on the other. It was exasperating. The situation only improved once we moved past that stage.

"Did you ever read adventure books as a kid?" She'd gone off on one of her usual tangents. Now didn't seem like the time for nostalgia, though.

I shrugged. I guess I had. Sally now had a familiar twinkle in her eye.

"I always wanted to try that trick to make the keys fall onto a piece of paper and pull them out."

I looked at the gap under the front door. It had always annoyed me but now it could save us from spending a fortune on a locksmith. From that moment on the blame game was over and we turned it into an old-fashioned mission to open that door in any way we could.

It took about two hours to go and buy the slimmest screwdriver we could find, spread out a newspaper under the closed door, and gently work the keys until they dropped onto the paper.

We did it. We opened the door and hugged each other triumphantly. Teamwork at its best!

The feeling of relief and achievement was amazing. We'd done something borderline miraculous by focusing on it and working together. If we'd just carried on blaming each other, who knows, maybe we'd still be standing outside that door right now. Well maybe not, but you get the point.

This is just one example of how time management and organization can become more complicated when ADHD is present. Here are some of the areas where I noted this was an issue at times.

- Finding it difficult to prioritize tasks
- Not taking responsibility for carrying out tasks
- A lot of time spent procrastinating and not getting started easily
- Difficulty in working out how long something will take and then how long has actually passed since starting
- Planning tasks is difficult
- Not following through on plans
- Losing track of time and getting distracted
- Not showing interest in planning and organizing
- Leaving it all to the other partner

My example earlier about the keys might seem more of a spur of the moment oversight, but it wouldn't have happened without the early issues where Sally lost her keys and forgot to get others cut. There's also the fact that we were racing out the door because we were already running late. So, I think a lot of problems can be traced back to this area even when it's not immediately related.

Take a moment to think about time issues you've had. I would imagine that plenty of them have their roots in ADHD. You'll find space in your Workbook to make notes on this. This is helpful because it lets us see where there are problems. So we know where to start looking for solutions.

Here's another bad memory where we can look for time management and organization issues that caused it. There was a concert we wanted to go to and see at the theater on the other side of the city. One of our favorite books had been made into a show and we were both excited about it.

Naturally, we wanted to get there early, eat something at a nearby restaurant, and enjoy the build-up. So why did we end up racing up the stairs, starving and stressed when the first act had already begun?

Let's rewind a few hours.

"I didn't realize you were going to get so dressed up tonight." She had a strange look in her eye when she said it.

"My tuxedo's at the dry cleaners, so this will have to do."

I mean, you don't normally get so smartly dressed to visit my family."

"Umm, are they starring in the show?"

"What show?"

After talking at cross-purposes for a few more minutes, the realization struck us. We'd been invited to Sally's parent's house but she hadn't checked the diary or asked me. Then she completely forgot to tell me.

ADHD COUPLES

I was getting ready for a big night in the theater district and she was getting ready for some family gossip and homemade cookies. Delicious homemade cookies to be fair, but that wasn't important right now.

I wanted to cancel but we didn't have the heart to let down her parents as they were going through a bad time. After wasting about 20 minutes arguing I wanted to draw up a plan to fit in both events but Sally wanted to just leave immediately and see what happened. It would work out fine, she told me.

We eventually did it her way, like we almost always did in these situations.

As you can imagine, everything that could possibly go wrong from that point onwards did go wrong. Traffic jams. No parking spaces. Her mother hadn't finished cooking when we got there. The biggest disaster? She hadn't made her famous chocolate chip cookies!

We eventually came clean and told them about our double booking for the evening. Her parents just laughed and told us to enjoy the show. We rushed across to the other city without eating any dinner and feeling totally stressed.

Thankfully, the show was fantastic but missing the first act was disappointing. To be honest, rushing about like this is bad for your health too. Apart from our blood pressure shooting through the roof, we could have crashed the car by rushing like that.

How To Resolve These Issues

The good news is that this should be easier to resolve than some of the other areas we've looked at. A lot of the ways of avoiding problems of this type are just common sense.

- Create a daily routine where you eat healthily and get enough exercise and sleep. We downloaded a fitness app that tracks our activity and includes healthy recipes. At the start of the week, we plan our meals so that we can buy everything we need at once.

- Carry out routine tasks at certain times of day or week. So maybe Sunday evening is for checking that bills are paid and double-checking your schedule for the week to make sure you're not overly committed.

- If you've got big tasks then break them down into smaller and more manageable chunks. Don't try to renovate the whole house. Start with a single wall in a single room and take it from there.

- Use reminders and alarms, for recurring tasks and also for special events that you can't afford to forget about. Make sure that you share the responsibility, so you both have the same alarm and reminders.

- Speak to each other. Again, good communication can stop a lot of issues from even happening in the first place.

If I think back to those two situations, there were several points in each of them where these points could have saved the day.

Prioritizing tasks and responsibilities is the next vital section. Some people are fantastic at prioritizing and just seem to be capable of working out what needs to be done next at any given time. But if your partner had ADHD then this is probably a struggle for them.

The first step is to prioritize together. Don't just do it all yourself and then hand over a list for your partner to stick to. It's far better to be together as you look at the tasks you need to do in the next week or month. That way you get their buy-in and it feels like something you're doing together.

Why is each one important? When is it really possible to do them? Are certain tasks dependent upon the completion of others? These are all great questions to ask yourself and each other.

I used to work on projects, so I use Gantt charts to do this. They look a bit daunting at first but they're easy to follow once you understand what you're looking at. But whatever format looks good to both of you is fine, as long as you both agree to it.

Mark the most urgent tasks. You can then separate the others that you don't need to do right away.

How do you rank the urgency? What are the consequences of a task not being completed on time? It might not seem like a big deal but what if missing it means getting a big bank charge or an important warranty running out? Other tasks might seem more important but missing the date doesn't really bring any serious consequences.

You then look at a realistic deadline for each one. Putting a deadline that's too soon is pointless. All you'll be doing is giving yourself twice the work as you'll need to schedule it again when the original deadline passes.

Making the deadline too far away is also a bad idea. At this point, I'd like to recall one of my favorite quotes.

 "Give me six hours to chop down a tree and I will spend the first four sharpening the ax." - Abraham Lincoln

That brings me nicely onto eating frogs. You see, 'Eating The Frog' is a time management concept and the name is inspired by a Mark Twain quote.

 "Eat a live toad the first thing in the morning and nothing worse will happen to you the rest of the day."

Start the day with your most difficult task. This will give you a sense of relief and let you look ahead to the rest of the day more confidently. At least there are no more toads ahead. You've got the worst part of your day out of the way and now you can concentrate on the rest.

Bear those wise quotes in mind when planning your tasks and they'll help you enormously.

You can now look at whether to break down the biggest tasks. Let's say you want to book a vacation. You'll need to work out a budget, check the latest deals, read some reviews, and book time off work. There's no reason to make this a single task.

Bear in mind what skills and interests you both have. For example, if we're looking for a vacation then Sally loves going to travel agencies and asking for details. But I prefer to look online for reviews and videos. So we can each concentrate on what suits us best. Then get together to discuss it.

By following these pieces of advice, you'll be working together to get more organized. There's absolutely no point in one of you being incredibly organized if the other one is terribly disorganized.

I'd like to go back for a second to the validation and empathy advice from the previous chapter. These are ways of communicating well that you should take into account in everything we cover from now on. Empathizing helps you to avoid blaming the other person for not being organized. It lets you look at the problems differently and wonder why this has happened. Isn't that a better way to view the issues between you and your partner?

Getting organized isn't about telling your partner what to do. It's about talking to each other and seeing what works for both of you. Do it well and you'll be on the right path to a less stressful life. You'll both feel that you're contributing to making this a healthier relationship.

Fail to get organized and your emotions will be all over the place. The emotional aspect of being in an ADHD-affected relationship is what I want to cover next anyway. So let's take a moment to consider the benefits of being well-organized before we take a deep breath and continue our emotional journey.

5

EVERYONE TAKE A DEEP BREATH!

How To Regulate The Emotional Journey Of ADHD

The idea that you have to be protected from any kind of uncomfortable emotion is what I absolutely do not subscribe to.

— John Cleese

If the experience of your own emotions is like a ride on a rollercoaster, this is the chapter where you'll learn the necessary practical tips to regulate your emotions.

One of the potentially damaging aspects of ADHD is that it makes it more difficult to keep your emotions under control. And if your emotions run wild then it's going to have an impact on your relationship.

Let's look at this logically. Emotions are contagious[18]. If one of you goes through massive peaks and troughs then the other will too. As with everything else we've explored here, you are in this together and good communication is the starting point.

We're seeking solid emotional control. That's the basis for a healthy, lasting relationship. Therefore, the first point we need to cover is why this matters.

- Good emotional control is a vital part of your own mental well-being.
- Emotional dysregulation in a couple can lead to impulsive behavior, attacks on the other partner, withdrawal from communication, misunderstandings, and the use of extreme language.

Even if this doesn't last long each time, it will probably take you a while to recover from each episode of emotional dysregulation. An argument can end up ruining your time spent together for a day, a week, or even longer.

The first step to resolving this issue lies in noticing there's a problem to deal with. If you tend to sweep your emotions under

Good emotional control is a vital part of your own mental well-being

ADHD COUPLES

the carpet then this situation can drag on for years, slowly poisoning your relationship.

Therefore, you can start by looking at the emotional needs[19] we all have in relationships. These range from affection to connection, space, and validation. If any of these areas are missing, it's going to make it incredibly difficult to maintain a loving and thoughtful relationship.

Have you asked them?

Do you know what your partner's emotional needs are? Do they understand yours? As a fascinating exercise in awareness, in your Workbook we've included a list of common emotional needs with the ability to rank them in importance. There is a list for you to complete and one for your partner to complete. Arrange a time to do this exercise and discover where you both align and where you may need to allow for differences in what each of you needs from the relationship to be emotionally satisfied.

What Impact Does ADHD Have On Emotional Needs?

- Someone with ADHD may experience overwhelming emotions[20]. Surveys have shown that emotional dysregulation is common in people with ADHD, so you need to be aware of this risk.

- The person with this condition may have problems controlling their emotional responses[21]

- They may find it difficult to explain to you how they're feeling

- They may have intense mood swings that their partner struggles to understand

- They might feel that their partner doesn't seem to take notice of how they feel

These are all serious issues. If your emotional needs aren't being met and this condition is sustained, the relationship is going to be unsatisfying.

Let's take a moment to look again at those points just mentioned. What does that look like in real-life situations?

- The overwhelming emotions that ADHD causes can lead to impulsive behavior. You're not going to be able to control your emotions if they get hit by wave after wave of intensity. This can feel like too much emotion for anyone and can also affect the person's partner.

- Sometimes, Sally would answer me with something really over the top and with an emotional reaction that I felt was out of proportion to the subject. I now realize that this was due to ADHD making it difficult for her to control her emotions.

- We often reached an impasse where Sally couldn't tell me what the problem was. She would get wound up about an issue and I never really understood what it was. It might be something that seemed really minor to me but she would get upset and I was confused as to why.

- The mood swings that are caused by an emotional imbalance can be disorienting. One moment your partner is laughing happily and the next it's all doom and gloom. This makes it difficult to relax and build trust.

How Does Emotional Dysregulation Affect Relationships?

By now it should be clear that this is a major issue. You risk losing your special connection, each of you lost in your own emotional ups and downs. You're on different emotional journeys to each other.

Emotions play a huge part in life. Can you imagine living without ever feeling happy or sad or angry or afraid? Living like an emotionless robot who doesn't feel soaring highs or sink to bottomless depths of despair?

Our emotions carry out various essential functions. They help us to act instinctively, such as when the fight or flight response kicks in. They influence how we think and they motivate us to modify our future behavior.

Without emotions, our lives would be very different. In particular, can you even begin to imagine a relationship devoid of emotion? This is impossible, but we need those emotions to be the right ones. Above all, we need to be in step with our partner's emotions.

If there is emotional dysregulation in your relationship, what is this going to mean? It's going to mean an inability to cope with the emotions you come across. You or your partner aren't going to react adequately to the emotions that arise during your life together.

Some Coping Strategies

This isn't the end of the road, as there are some powerful coping strategies you can adopt. There are ways of regulating your emotions that have been proven to work for many couples. Not every strategy is right for everyone, so give them a try and see which ones suit you best.

Mindfulness techniques are excellent for helping you to reflect and develop a greater sense of self-awareness. Many people use them as a way of reducing stress but they also help you to self-regulate your emotions by training your mind to look inwards.

Cognitive-behavioral therapy techniques can be used to manage your emotional responses too. This is a way of identifying problems and retraining your mind to turn negative thoughts into positive thoughts. You will become aware of the damaging thought patterns that you need to change and discover new behaviors that you can use instead.

This is typically carried out with the guidance of a therapist, although you will also find advice online on how to do it alone. It ties in with the stress reduction and relaxation techniques that we'll be looking at in a moment too.

Don't look at this like something boring or to be avoided. Rather, it's an exciting way of changing your way of thinking that could make you see life in an entirely fresh, new way.

 Change the way you think and you'll change the way you live.

Among the most exciting methods of doing this is cognitive restructuring. It's typically done with a therapist because it's difficult for anyone to spot their own problematic thought processes. Some of the issues that can be uncovered here include overgeneralizing, personalizing, and catastrophizing. Overly black-and-white thinking is another issue that you might find needs to be fixed.

 For context and some practical, real-life examples, see your Workbook where you'll also have the chance to practice this technique.

Techniques For Managing Stress And Anxiety

You've almost certainly seen some studies about stress lately. Headlines scream statistics like 74% of people have been overwhelmed by stress[22] in the last year or 87% of people call rising prices a major source of stress[23].

We live in a world where the mere thought of stress is enough to cause us stress.

Stress has become normalized. Saying you're stressed is an everyday phrase. We've forgotten what it's like to live without stress.

It wasn't meant to be like this. The stress you feel isn't "normal". So you need to, first of all, think about what triggers it. That study I mentioned earlier puts the cost of living ahead of global instability and wars. Stress is a very personal problem and we each get affected by different triggers.

Maybe your journey to work on a crowded train stresses you. Or driving and getting stuck in traffic. Or it's the customers you deal with at work. Or your home life. Or what you see on the news at night. Stress triggers are all around us and we can't change the world. But what we can do is change how we react to them.

Take a moment to consider what your key stress triggers are. If you aren't sure, take notes during the day as you feel your stress levels increase. This will let you work out what situations are getting you stressed. You'll find space and helpful prompts in your Workbook to make these notes.

The next step is to do something about it. You need coping strategies that stop stress and anxiety from overwhelming you.

Relaxation techniques including deep breathing and progressive muscle relaxation are excellent at helping lower stress. The deep breathing exercises in the Workbook are a simple way of getting started. You just need to spend as little as five minutes a day on it at the beginning. Then work your way up to do it for longer if you feel that it works for you.

Progressive muscle relaxation can be done in about 15 minutes per session following the guidelines in the Workbook. The secret to doing this well is to set aside enough time to do it comfortably and without any distractions. Do it right and you'll feel fantastic afterwards.

Any kind of exercise can also help, as we've seen in previous chapters. Why not try something new, whether it's tai chi, swimming, or dancing? You might find that a certain type of exercise helps you to feel more relaxed, or that it's a combination of different types that helps you most. Ideally, it'll be something you can do together. This gives you valuable time together while doing something incredibly useful.

ADHD COUPLES

Doing these exercises should be fun, but what about those daily tasks that aren't so enjoyable? We're talking about chores here and they can cause a huge amount of conflict. The question of who does the dishes and takes out the garbage can cause any couple to get frayed. So what should couples with ADHD know to stop this turning into a ticking time bomb? Find out in the next chapter.

IT'S YOUR TURN TO DO THE DISHES

Managing The Chores Without One Person Doing It All

Alone we can do so little, together we can do so much.

– Helen Keller

The chores that need to be carried out in your home aren't particularly exciting. No one rushes home to wash the dishes or counts the minutes until they can do the ironing. Yet, this is one of the most crucial aspects of family life.

Why is this? The simple fact is that dividing chores is a hassle in every home. You don't think that other couples happily decide who takes out the trash and who organizes the bedroom, do you?

80% of couples argue about chores[25], and almost none of them are asking their partner to let them do more. So, this is a sensitive subject in virtually every home. When one of the partners has ADHD, what does this mean?

DIVISION OF CHORES AND TASKS IN RELATIONSHIPS AFFECTED BY ADHD

A common feature in this sort of relationship is that one partner takes on more than their fair share of chores. Bearing in mind what we've covered so far, it's easy to imagine who ends up doing the most. That's right, the partner of the person who experiences ADHD is likely to do more than 50%.

That might not seem like a problem at first. Washing a few extra dishes isn't such a big deal, is it? Ironing more than your fair share isn't the end of the world. Shouldn't we be focusing on more important issues and forgetting this area?

Well, it might be fine at first. But what happens after you've been doing this for a few weeks or months? This is something that could become your routine for the rest of your life. That's years and years of doing extra chores. Suddenly, it seems a more serious subject when we look at it like this.

Feelings of resentment and frustration are likely to bubble up over time. We're all human and we all have a limit. That limit might be reached sooner for you than for others, or it might take longer. But you'll get there eventually, believe me.

I got sick of the sight of dirty dishes, dirty clothes, and bags of garbage. Sally never deliberately left these chores for me. It was just another example of the way that ADHD causes people to overlook or forget what they should be doing.

It can be overwhelming after a while. So, I think the first step is to approach this with an open mind. You need to communicate with your partner. You might be tempted to brush it under the carpet and pretend it's no big deal. In that case, just remember what I said about it turning into a big problem eventually. Because I promise you that day will come unless you do something about it.

SOME SUGGESTED STRATEGIES

The first point to bear in mind is that you need to give this area a lot of thought. Try different approaches until you find something that works. That's what we did and it worked well, but the solution didn't arrive overnight.

You'll find your own challenges and successes over time. But by following the ideas I tried out, you'll be off to a much better start.

The following are some of the tips you could try.

Find The Priority Tasks

You should work out what the most important tasks are in your home. This means you won't feel overwhelmed by a huge list of tasks. You can then focus on those important chores and gradually add others to the list.

Let's say that you plan to tidy out the spare room, put some plants in the garden, and get the car fixed. While these are all worthwhile jobs, most people are probably going to make getting the car fixed their top priority. But what if you work at home? Maybe getting the spare room ready to use as a home office is more important for you in that situation.

Every home and family is different, so don't just go by what other people class as *their* priorities. You need to take the time to work out your priorities. By doing that, you can see what needs to be done first.

Don't forget that you'll get a boost from completing any task. So if you make your priority something relatively fast and simple, this will give you the encouragement you need to move on to the next one.

Find A Routine That Suits You

Ideally, you'll work out a way to carry out the chores that fits your work and lifestyle. You don't want this to mean a huge change in your life, as that's when you can get stressed and resentful.

Big changes can be upsetting. If you need to stop a favorite hobby or get up an hour earlier because of chores, that's going to cause you negative feelings about this change in your life. On the other hand, if the routine is a positive change, or at least doesn't cause you problems, then the changes won't seem too bad to you.

So this is a way of lowering your stress levels. Or at least stopping them from increasing. And that's important because you want to enter this new phase of your life in a positive frame of mind.

Could it also help you to become more productive? It could be an opportunity to introduce some changes that help you work smarter.

For instance, you might want to set aside certain times of day for doing different chores. It might be a chance to organize your life better. It's then a question of making sure that you stick to the new routine as closely as you can but modify it if something isn't working.

Break Up Your Tasks As Much As You Can

Looking at a list of big tasks can be daunting. So you should find it easier to get going if you have a list covering shorter, easier chores.

This is human nature. We hate seeing that we've got difficult things to do. But if the list has easier tasks on it you might feel more comfortable with it. If you need to clean the house then take it one room at a time. If you need to make the garden prettier then you could choose a section to start with.

Use Good Communication Strategies

You need your partner to stay on track with what you're trying to do. The only way to do this is through good communication. We've already covered the importance of communicating and this is another example of how it's necessary in everyday life.

There's no benefit to creating a smart plan to carry out household chores if your partner doesn't know about it. Bearing in mind the communication issues we've looked at earlier, this is a crucial point.

It could get frustrating at times but try to stay positive and give encouragement rather than getting into arguments. Remember the validation and empathy points from earlier. Your partner could struggle to get used to the new way of living. But you're there to help.

How Can You Work As A Team?

Can you see how this is a fantastic opportunity to work together? The fact is that you can use this as a way to show your commitment to working as a team. This helps both of you. Rather than feeling all alone with the household chores, you could discover a new way of doing the tasks together. You'll both feel that you're contributing to the well-being of the partnership by taking part in the chores.

Good teamwork can bring you closer and may you both feel the benefits. It isn't going to be easy, though. This is why you need some team working strategies that you can use to get the chores done fairly and without either of you feeling hard done by.

- Look at your individual strengths. Both of you probably have different strengths. One of you might be great at organizing the house while the other is better at cooking or cleaning. Understanding these differences makes it easier to divide the tasks fairly and in a way that makes sense.

- Play to your strengths while being open about taking on anything else if needed.

- Make it fair. Even if you want to do more than your fair share, the ideal approach is to make it 50/50. This is sustainable and it shows that you want to divide the work evenly. A 50/50 split is going to stand the test of time and make you both feel good about it.

- Be flexible and open-minded. There's a good chance that you end up with some chores that you don't like. That's a normal situation and not something to worry about. It's where you need to realize that you need to be flexible and take on tasks you don't want to do. If both of you adopt this attitude, it greatly improves the chances of success.

- Be supportive and encouraging. This new way of dealing with chores is going to be a challenge for both of you. The best way of dealing with it is by supporting one another at all times. There may be difficult moments ahead but try to make the overall process smoother by praising and helping your partner at every possible opportunity.

EXAMPLES OF HOW IT COULD WORK

Right now, you might be wondering how this could possibly work. Carrying out chores has possibly become a major problem in your home. So you've decided to take it all on yourself.

This is what I did for a while. I just thought that life would be easier if I silently washed the dishes in the evening and then took out the garbage. I'd put our clothes in the washing machine at the weekend and tidy the house whenever I had a spare moment.

I don't want you to think that Sally didn't do anything. She quite likes washing clothes and tidying up in the garden, for example. But she didn't have a routine. So if I saw a big pile of dirty clothes or overgrown weeds, I'd just do it myself.

In this way, our house was always reasonably tidy. But I was exhausted and resentful. It all came to a head one day when I couldn't find any clean towels. I'd been working extra hours during the week so I hadn't been able to do much housework. The place was a mess.

I eventually found the wet, used towels under a pile of clothing. I felt so frustrated. I'd been working like crazy to keep this house ticking over. But a few days where I hadn't done everything and it was a disaster zone.

Looking back now, I can see that it was an overreaction. Yet, I think this shows how resentment builds up over time. I wasn't angry because the towels hadn't been washed. I was angry because I'd been washing them all the time. And the first time I dropped the ball Sally hadn't been there to pick it up.

Once things settled down, I went through that process we looked at a moment ago. When I spoke to Sally, she was really good about it. She had been feeling awful about not helping out around the house anyway. She just didn't know how to start a conversation about it.

We can see once again how crucial communication is. If there's no communication then everything breaks down. As soon as we started talking about what to do, the pieces fell into place. There's no magic formula, other than talking to one another sensibly.

We start by creating a weekly schedule like the one you can see in the Workbook. We could then work on slotting in our names next to each task.

Sally claimed the garden and the laundry like I knew she would. But things were going to be different this time. First, we broke it down into tasks. This means that we had a big laundry session at the weekend when our work clothes and everything else that had built up during the week got done. But there was also a mid-week session for catching up with towels, bedsheets, and anything else that was running short and couldn't wait until the weekend.

The gardening tasks, we broke into sections. The first week was weeding, and Sally said she could do that on Sunday morning when the warm sun on her face made this a pleasure. We added in my task of washing the car at the same time. So there was virtually no chance of either of us forgetting our tasks. The other gardening tasks were then slotted neatly into the remaining weeks of the month.

In this way, we went through the rest of the chores, looking for areas where one of us wanted to take on the responsibility. We ended up turning it into a game of bingo and it was really useful for me to get the weight off my shoulders.

At the end of the session, we had a schedule that made sense for both of us. I'm not going to pretend that carrying out household chores suddenly became a delight. I didn't rush home to wash the dishes or have a spring in my step when I washed the shampoo off the car.

But the big difference was that we both felt we were in this together. Sally said that she no longer felt guilty about leaving everything to me. And I felt more relaxed because I knew we were sharing these tasks.

CARRY OUT THE BORING CHORES AND ENJOY THE GOOD TIMES

Being in a relationship isn't just about the good times. It would be great if life with a partner only involved going out for a drink then getting a pizza delivered and enjoying a movie. But someone's got to throw out that pizza box and pay the streaming service subscription. If no one's tidied the living room then the sofa will be filled with clothes and plates and who knows what other debris we leave behind in our daily lives.

Therefore, for me, the best way of looking at chores is as a necessary evil. Someone has to do it. And leaving it all to one person in the relationship is going to cause problems sooner or later. This is why you should make the effort to follow those steps above and find the most painless way of carrying out the chores together.

It might seem like a pretty minor point. But believe me, it's going to make a difference to the quality of your lives.

We're moving in the right direction now, but there are still some important areas to cover. The first of them is no laughing matter.

It's about the money that a person with ADHD might struggle to use well.

That means it's time to get serious about cash now. Read on and see if you can relate to many of the situations I'm going to write about in your life.

WAIT. YOU BOUGHT WHAT?!

Effective Money Management

Don't tell me what your priorities are. Show me where you spend your money and I'll tell you what they are.

– James W. Frick

Money is a huge part of every relationship. If one of you doesn't look after your cash, it's going to cause problems and frustrations for the other. I made the mistake of not being open about my money worries with my partner. I thought these problems would sort themselves out but they didn't. They never do. If you're going to get into a better financial situation then it'll be through doing the right things and talking about it.

Let's talk about money ...

CHALLENGES WITH MONEY MANAGEMENT

This is one area where you might not think that ADHD matters. Surely this condition doesn't affect your finances as well as everything else we've looked at?

Sadly, money worries can be a big part of dealing with ADHD in your relationship. If it's not happening to you yet then I'll show you what to avoid. And if you're currently struggling then we'll explore some strategies to get your finances back on track.

Let's start with the main reasons why this matters. There are four categories where ADHD causes money problems.

Impulsivity Leading To Overspending

This was a big problem for us. Sally didn't spend fortunes on luxury vacations or designer clothes. But she didn't have a sensible, forward-looking approach either.

Let me give you an example. It was January - the toughest month of the year - a week before we both got paid and our funds were running low. I'm sure most people have been there a few times. You're trying to save money in any way you can. Making sandwiches to take to work with you. Walking to work and back. All simple little things that aren't that difficult.

But then I got home and found that Sally had ordered takeaway food for us. It was an attempt to break the routine and enjoy a nice evening. The idea was good but it wasn't the right time for it. She hadn't thought about how we were going to pay for this and make it to the end of the month as well.

I couldn't enjoy the pasta as much as I normally would, even with the spicy sauce that she knows I love. Because I was thinking about how every mouthful was costing us money we didn't have in our accounts. At the end of the meal, she noticed that I was quiet and we got into an argument about how I was too boring. I was furious because I felt that I was the only one taking this relationship seriously.

The last few days before getting paid were awful. We had to get creative with our meals and walk everywhere, Yet, somehow we both see it as kind of fun when we look back now. We created some kind of potato and beans mashup dish that we still joke about today. But at the time it was no laughing matter.

Disorganization And Forgetfulness

We've already looked at some examples of Sally forgetting to pay bills and get financial tasks carried out on time. It's something that really puzzled me for years. How could such a smart woman with a good job forget to pay the rent or the internet bill on time?

If I hadn't discovered the truth about ADHD, I'd have thought that she simply didn't care. In fact, that's what I eventually thought at the time. Why else would someone risk us losing our home or getting into financial problems when it was easily avoided?

Procrastination And Avoidance

This wasn't a big deal in our relationship, but I can see how it could be a major issue for other couples. With so many thoughts in her mind, it would have been easy for Sally to put off paying bills. But she usually just clean forgot about them, so procrastination was never much of a problem.

In terms of avoiding her financial responsibility, I can see that was definitely part of it. Sally never wanted to sit down and talk to me about saving for the future. I know now what this was, but once again I saw it at the time as a lack of interest in our future.

The best advice is to look out for signs of procrastination. Are the bills piling up? Has your partner still not opened that savings account they said they would open? Are there other signs that they need help in this aspect?

Financial Stress And Conflict

Like most couples, we started out earning relatively low salaries and then started working our way up the corporate ladder. After a couple of years, we were both earning well and lived in a nice flat. There's no way we should have been struggling at the end of the month. Or having to eat bizarre potato and bean hybrid dishes.

So, I think ADHD put us under more financial pressure than would otherwise have been the case. And this caused us to argue over money when we probably wouldn't have otherwise.

Every couple has a different situation in this respect. However, I'm sure that ADHD causes many couples to have more money issues than would otherwise have been the case. I read that billions of dollars are lost every year in workplaces due to untreated ADHD[30]. People struggling with this condition might also find it more difficult to get and keep a good job.

STRATEGIES FOR BUDGETING AND FINANCIAL PLANNING

So far, we've seen a few problems that I expect most couples with ADHD can relate to. The big question now is what solutions they can find. I've been reflecting on how we got back on track and the following are the key points I want to share with you.

Create A Budget That Works For Both Partners

Put all your monthly income and outgoing into a spreadsheet. You can then see at a glance whether you earn more than you spend. From that point on, you work out how you're going to budget each month.

Everyone has their own way of doing this, as we all have different lifestyles and tastes. The most important point is that you write it all down. Because this is about taking back control of your finances. You don't want any nasty surprises at the end of the month.

If you get into the habit of revising the budget, there's far less chance of anything being overlooked. You can then refine it over time and work out more precisely how much you need to put aside each month for different reasons.

Financial apps are good for letting you track your finances easily. But I found that actually sitting down together and typing everything into a spreadsheet was great. The aspect of physically typing it with a keyboard seemed to help us take it more seriously.

I've shared all of the information we use to create our budgets in the Workbook so you can pick up the habit too. Go there at the end of this chapter to get started.

Tracking Expenses And Income

The best part of the previous idea is that you can track your expenses and income as often as you want to. This means that there's far less risk of a nasty surprise catching you off guard.

Doing this is a good idea for everyone. And it's essential for couples with ADHD. As soon as we started tracking out money, the situation improved. We could make the cash stretch to the end of the month more easily, as we were more relaxed too. This meant that there were far fewer arguments over money in our home.

Setting Financial Goals And Priorities

Everything we've looked at so far is great for getting by month to month. Paying the bills and having food in the fridge will keep you from getting stressed before payday. But we know there's more to life than that.

ADHD COUPLES

You want to save up to go on vacation. Maybe you want to buy a car or a house. If you're planning on starting a family then that takes a lot of money too.

This means that setting your financial goals is crucial. In my experience, this will also help both of you to feel more together and focused on building a strong future. You're both committing to the relationship and saying that you're going to do all you can to make it work now and in the future.

This is the type of plan that needs you to sit down and discuss the details in a relaxed manner. We did it one day. We went for a drive and took a picnic with us. The weather was threatening to ruin the day, as the sky was filled with menacing clouds that looked like they would open up and soak us at any moment.

Still, we unpacked our little wicker basket of sandwiches and fruit. We laid out our blankets and put the radio on low. Classic rock. Perfect for the occasion.

It was good to be away from the city for a while and I was feeling more relaxed than I had been in some time. As for Sally, getting out into the countryside is one of the best ways of getting her to focus. She looked happy and I could tell that the time was right to have a deep conversation about money.

I started by mentioning a few of my dreams for the future and held my breath as I hoped that Sally would confirm that she had the same ones. She did, and this led to us getting excited about how we could make them come true.

We all know that you need money to make dreams come true. This means that we needed to work out what was most important to us, and then see how to achieve it.

It's a very personal issue for every couple and I suggest taking the time to get it right. The rain eventually caused us to pack up and go home. But by then we'd already started about our plans for the future.

Building An Emergency Fund

You never know when you might get hit by an emergency like illness, losing your job, or your car breaking down. All of these problems are going to stretch your finances, which is why having an emergency fund is vital.

How much should you squirrel away for emergencies? The best advice I can share is that you should have three to six months of expenses covered[31]. This is where your budgeting from earlier is going to be useful. You already know how much you need each month, so those same figures are what you need here.

If you can save more than six months of expenses then all the better. You might consider this if either of you is in unstable employment or there is some other risk factor such as an underlying medical condition.

The next point is how to do this. You might want to use a savings app that prompts you to put away a certain amount each month. Or set up an automated payment from your main bank account to your savings account.

One trick I learned was to keep the savings in an account that isn't very easy to access. This can mean one that requires you to advise in advance that you want to take money out. Or you could just make it slightly awkward in terms of setting up two-factor authentication and an unusual password.

Since the big problem here is impulsivity, the most important point is that you want to stop rash decisions. If the person with ADHD has an extra few minutes to think about it, the urge might pass without a purchase being made.

Bear in mind that money problems are among the main factors in disputes among couples. It's the third-leading cause of divorce[32]. But the good news is that committed couples tend to be financially more successful.

Therefore, you have twice as many reasons for making this work. If you can sort out your financial issues and work together, you can remove one of the biggest reasons for splitting up. And you'll also be giving yourselves the best chance of succeeding.

Look at it this way. If you can get into a good financial situation, you'll feel that nothing can stop you. Don't sleepwalk into major issues when you can work with your partner for a bright future.

Planning For Major Expenses

Isn't it annoying when a major expense hits you out of the blue? We've all been there. You think your finances are under control, There's no longer any reason to avoid reading your bank statement. But then a huge expense blindsides you. If only you'd seen it coming ...

To start this section, we need to separate these expenses into two categories. The first covers unexpected expenses that I couldn't have planned for. This is when your car breaks down out of the blue. Or when a storm damages your house. Or one of you gets sick. You had no way of knowing this would happen.

These are situations that the emergency fund has to cover. If anything like this happens before you have an emergency fund, it's going to be tough. But once you've put away some cash, it'll make life easier.

This leaves us with the second expense. It's the kind of situation where you've completely forgotten about it until the time comes to pay for it. An insurance policy premium, scheduled car maintenance, or something of that sort,

You kick yourself because you know that you should have had it under control. You messed up.

This can be avoided by being organized. On those spreadsheets we mentioned earlier, you can add the annual expenses. Divide them into the appropriate months and you'll always see what is due next. This also gives you the chance to see if you can pay in instalments or find a cheaper deal before it's too late.

With this part of our lives together sorted out, it's time to enjoy ourselves. In the next chapter, we'll be looking at intimacy and sexuality. It's a lot more exciting than carrying out chores but there are more potential pitfalls to avoid as well. So let's turn the lights down low and see how you and your partner can enjoy a more satisfying and trouble-free time together.

NOT TONIGHT, BABE

Enhancing Your Intimacy And Sexuality

Intimacy is about truth. When you realize you can tell someone your truth, when you can show yourself to them, when you stand in front of them and their response is 'you're safe with me', that's intimacy.

– Taylor Jenkins Reid

I had doubted whether to include this chapter. After all, it's an extremely sensitive subject and not everyone is comfortable reading about intimacy between partners.

Then I remembered how many problems this subject had caused between Sally and me. I would say that this was probably our number one issue at one point. It's such an important part of life in a relationship that I simply couldn't leave it out. But how was I going to approach such a delicate matter?

Sally noticed that I was spending a lot of time in front of the laptop without typing anything.

"Are you nearly finished with the book?"

"Yeah, I'm at a … .sensitive part."

"Oh, you mean you're at the sexy bit?"

"How did you guess? It's kind of difficult."

"Tell them about that time we–"

I jumped in to interrupt her.

"I'd rather focus on practical advice if you don't mind."

"Then tell them about that time you walked out ."

"I already started the book with that."

"Did you? But did you explain everything about how we'd lost our spark? You didn't, did you? You can't leave that out."

Ok, so we need to go back to the beginning. You'll remember that I was walking out and leaving Sally. This wasn't a decision I had taken lightly. I hope I've been able to get across by this point that we're really in love. We have always been in love, even during the difficult times. But some challenges in life just seem too big at first.

I have to admit that our lack of intimacy was one of the major reasons we had drifted apart. I'm not talking just about sexual activity here. I mean those nights when we would snuggle up in bed and watch a sad movie. Or when we'd go out on a date night and pretend we'd just met. Or those times when we shared a secret joke and everyone else just looked at us like we were crazy.

To go from being like a couple of teenagers giddily in love to becoming people who hardly spent time together was hard to take. We both just wanted to turn back the clock and live in our own love bubble again.

It took me a long time to realize that real life isn't like that. What we'd experienced once was amazing and unforgettable. But if we wanted that level of intimacy again we needed to work at it and be practical. And of course, ADHD was there to make things more difficult.

So I decided to make a plan to get Sally back. It didn't rely on flowers and chocolates. Instead, the old romantic in me was going to woo her with spreadsheets and plans.

CHALLENGES WITH INTIMACY AND SEXUALITY IN RELATIONSHIPS AFFECTED BY ADHD

The starting point here has to be - once again - solid communication. I know we've covered it already but let's look at it in a new light. We now need to consider communication in terms of the emotional connection between a couple.

This isn't the same as communicating that dinner's ready or that it's time to weed the garden. It's that feeling of connecting on a deeper level so that you both feel completely comfortable with one another. If your relationship once had this and lost it then you know exactly how bad I was feeling.

There are a few key points to consider here.

- People with ADHD may struggle in terms of verbal communication. This is a big part of intimacy, as it provides the platform for feeling relaxed and for opening up to the other.

- A variety of speech and language issues can be among the symptoms for those with ADHD[26], so you need to understand that. Remember our point earlier about empathy? Your partner is likely to be just as frustrated as you are if their ADHD makes it difficult for them to maintain an emotional connection through good communication.

- There's no simple answer to this, but the communication strategies we covered in Chapter 3 provide a solid starting point. Just bear in mind that they aren't only for communicating about practical matters. You also need to use your improved communication skills to help create intimacy as a couple. Try looking at those key points around validation and empathy in this light.

Keeping The Emotional Connection Alive

The next term I want to discuss is emotional disconnection. This follows on from the last section, as good communication will keep your bond strong and allow you to keep that tight connection every couple needs.

Anyone with ADHD suffers the risk of being emotionally detached, and there are some medications that may even exacerbate this feeling[27].

They may become more emotionally detached at difficult or stressful times. This is because the condition makes it hard for them to regulate their emotions. Naturally, this has an impact on how well they can connect with a partner on an emotional level.

Again, to find a solution we need to go back to an earlier chapter. In this case, Chapter 5 gives us details of how to make our emotional journey smoother. There are plenty of practical points and strategies there to get you started.

As with the communication section. I'd encourage you to go back and read it now in a new light. Consider how you can build your emotional connection in these ways, creating a new bond of intimacy between you.

Now, we can consider both of these points together. How can you use better communication to help control your emotions? This comes from understanding your own personality and your partner's. What are the key challenges that stop you from getting closer and how can you use solid communication to overcome them?

Time To Talk About Physical Intimacy

You might think that ADHD doesn't really have any effect on physical intimacy. Yet, there are some powerful reasons for believing that it's definitely a factor.

If one of you has ADHD, this person is possibly going to have problems with impulsivity and hyperactivity. This is something that affects many aspects of life and there are reasons to believe that your sex life is among them.

What are some of the common issues to look out for?

- Difficulty in paying attention during moments of intimacy. It may be difficult for the affected partner to focus. This means that their mind may wander even during sex and other intimate moments such as when you're alone and cuddling. There's no doubt this is a worry for the other partner. They'll probably see it as a lack of interest in the physical side of the relationship.

- We've mentioned emotional swings and mood changes earlier. This is another common symptom that can affect a person's level of interest in physical intimacy. Something that they're comfortable with one day might seem annoying the next day.

- Other feelings can get in the way of your relationship. Those with ADHD and their partners may feel isolated and lonely at times. This is likely to stop them from achieving a strong level of intimacy.

- The impulsiveness associated with certain types of ADHD is another potential issue. This can lead to the person taking risky decisions that affect their love life. Finding a stable, tender relationship might be what they really want, but controlling their impulsive urges won't be easy.

- Taking certain medications can make any of these points more likely to occur. It's impossible to predict what exact effect these treatments will have on a person. It might help them control their ADHD in other ways but cause issues for you in the bedroom.

Tips For Getting Back Your Intimacy

If you lose the physical intimacy in a relationship then getting it back has to be a priority as sex can play a huge part in our lives with a partner.

Don't just accept that this part of your life together is gone. And don't just let it carry on, in the hope that the situation sorts itself out. This is a problem that needs to be fixed. And the sooner the better. Let's take a look at some of the ideas you could consider to achieve this.

Okay, so we'll start with the communication aspect, yet again. That's fine because it reinforces how important it is in *every* aspect of life. You can't have good communication the rest of the time and then let it disappear when the lights are out.

Make it a subject you can both talk about. Sex shouldn't be taboo in any relationship. It's even more important that you talk about it when there's ADHD to deal with. Being open about this aspect will help you both to relax and feel that you're in it together.

If one of you has trouble focusing then don't make it into *that thing we can't talk about*. It will just get worse and you'll both get more uptight if you try and put a lid on it. Take off the lid and examine it together. It's your sex life and only you can work out how to make it better.

Like everything else we've considered here, this is no one's fault. ADHD has reared its head in your relationship and you're both trying to deal with it as best you can.

Encourage your partner to tell you what they're thinking and what they want. If you both do this, you lower the risk of misunderstandings that get in the way of those tender moments.

Removing any distractions from the place where you spent time together is another good move. In a lot of cases, this can be as simple as turning off the light and turning off the TV when you go to bed. In other cases, you might need to consider whether to make some changes to the room. Maybe you can use heavier curtains or turn it into a minimalist bedroom. Some soft music perhaps? Whatever floats your boat and rocks your socks is fine.

Let's go back to the medication issue again. We've seen that there are several recommended types of medication that could help with the symptoms. But in specific cases, they might or might not have the desired effect.

Specifically, you might find that the medication either helps you to focus and enjoy the physical side of the relationship. Or that it dampens your appetite and causes problems in maintaining a healthy relationship.

If you feel that the drugs you or your partner have been prescribed are harming your sex life, you need to speak to your doctor. There may be something else you can try that doesn't have this effect. Don't hide it from your partner either. Get the subject out in the open and encourage your partner to speak freely about this crucial part of your life together.

How To Keep Relaxed And On Track

One of the issues with sexual problems is that we can quickly get desperate to fix them. Which tends to only make matters worse.

There's no doubt that ADHD can make it difficult for couples to get intimate. This can come in a number of ways, such as physical difficulty in getting aroused or reaching orgasm.

It's a situation that can easily lead to confusion and misunderstanding. You both want things to go back to normal but it's just getting worse instead. The more you focus on sex, the more difficult it gets. It's like going around in circles and getting increasingly exasperated.

There's no simple answer to this problem. But what we can do is change the focus. Let's look at how you can start to enjoy your intimate time together again.

- Don't make it all about sex. Instead of applying pressure, you should relax and just enjoy your time together. This means taking time to enjoy intimate moments together but without the end goal always being sex. There are plenty of other ways you can kiss, cuddle, and enjoy each other's bodies while recovering your confidence.

- Stay fit and healthy. If your lifestyle isn't particularly active, this could be having a negative impact on your sex life too. Exercising regularly is a fantastic way of feeling good and getting in the mood for some intimacy. If you work out together then that's even better.

- Consider therapy as an option. Talking to an expert can take a huge weight off your mind. A therapist can help you to deal with this situation in the right way. If you're struggling to bring up the subject with your partner, this could be a way to get started.

What Strategies Can Build Intimacy Between Partners?

You should now be feeling more comfortable with the idea of trying again to build some intimacy. As mentioned earlier, it was something that had drifted out of our relationship and I wanted to get it back.

To do this, I decided to come up with some strategies that could help us. I'll list them here so that you can see them side by side and decide which ones might be best for you.

- Better communication. This was the biggest and most important change in our relationship. Improving our communication certainly wasn't easy, as it had broken down completely by the time I left. This was the time for action. So I put into action the points we've looked at in the communication chapter. We were both hurting and it took time. But eventually, techniques like empathy and validation started to bring us together.

- Make the effort to spend time together. One of our problems, as we drifted apart, was that we started spending less time together. This made it difficult for us to recover that intimate feeling of being together. To put it bluntly, we had started becoming more like a pair of arguing friends than lovers. We needed to spend more time together.

- Find activities you both like. Following on from the last point, I felt that we needed to find activities we both enjoyed. We could then spend time together having fun. This is when we started walking together. The first couple of times were kind of awkward. By the third time, we'd started holding hands. By the fifth or sixth time, we stopped in our new favorite spot for some kissing time. The plan was working.

- Show more affection. The walking trips turned into more adventurous affairs. And the further we went from home, the more affectionate we became. At first, I had to make an effort to take Sally's hand and touch her cheek and so on. After a while, it became second nature again. We could forget about ADHD and other problems while we strolled together. We were just a couple of people happy to spend time together again.

- Don't fall into a routine. Once walking became a routine, we switched to cycling. This kept things fresh and forced us to look for different ways to rebuild our bond. It was perfect because we would cycle side by side but couldn't hold hands or anything. So we were both keen for some physical contact by the time we arrived. The important point here is to not fall into a routine that undoes the good work so far.

- Give compliments. This is one of the simplest ways of building trust and intimacy with your partner. Yet, it was something I'd never really done before. The time I'd taken to get my plan to recover my relationship in action let me see that it was necessary. I didn't go overboard, but I tried to make Sally feel appreciated. Isn't it amazing how often we take the person we love most for granted? Start paying nice, genuine compliments and you'll be putting your relationship back on track.

- Try something completely different and new. Going around in circles trying to get the spark back isn't going to work. I know because I've been there. So try something new. Take a weekend break somewhere you've never been. Or just drive there on a day trip. Cook a romantic meal using interesting new ingredients. Go and watch a movie together. Climb to the top of that hill. Ride that boat. It doesn't have to be earth-shattering, just something that opens your mind to new things. This means it's going to distract you from problems and ADHD for a while.

ADHD And Sexual Dysfunction

Studies show that ADHD sufferers have higher rates of sexual dysfunction in several areas[29]. This includes higher rates of sexually transmitted diseases and lower satisfaction levels. Those with ADHD tend to indulge in risky behavior according to the study, although it also points out that there's a relative lack of research in the area.

The causes are all the factors we looked at near the beginning of the book. Impulsiveness, getting distracted, getting bored easily, losing interest. Each of these issues can have a knock-on effect on every part of life. It's no surprise to see that this includes sexual activity.

In fact, it would be pretty amazing if ADHD *didn't* damage your sex life. After all, it causes damage to so many other aspects of your life. Why should this part escape?

You want to make your relationship more satisfying for both of you. This means looking for solutions, and there are a few worth considering.

- Speak to a professional sex therapist. These counselors can help you to understand the situation. They're experienced in dealing with the emotional side of sex-related problems and can help you work through them more effectively.

- Try new things. If your intimacy has ground to a halt maybe it's time to reset the physical side of the relationship and start again. What could you try to get things going again? Maybe something new and challenging like tantric techniques. Or perhaps just new positions and forms of intimacy. There's a world of information out there and it would be great if you and your partner were willing to explore it together.

- Take care of yourself. If you're feeling good and in excellent health, your sexual well-being should take care of itself. Look after what you eat and the exercises you carry out. Try and stay positive about the challenges you're up against. This might not be enough on its own to put you back on the road to a better physical relationship but it's a great start.

Sorting out the physical side of your relationship is going to help you feel more relaxed and positive. This isn't the end of the story by any means. There's still a long road ahead of you.

In our case, we feel that we've turned a corner but that there's a lot still to do. This is a great feeling, as it gives us the incentive to go on and make the rest of our life together better.

Now seems like a great time to recap some of the things we've shared here and show exactly how you can put them into practice.

9

CREATING A BRILLIANT RELATIONSHIP

Strategies To Thrive Despite The Challenges

Far too many people are looking for the right person, instead of trying to be the right person.

– Gloria Steinem

We started this book with someone walking away. We're now going to end it with someone who is planning to stay.

Relationships are rarely easy. I'm sure you've seen a couple that looked perfect but you later found out that they're struggling or breaking up? So, I'm not going to promise that Sally and I will be together forever. Our lives just may not take that path.

But, I realized many things while writing this book. One was just how deeply in love we are. All that we've struggled through and achieved together, none of it would be possible without a deep sense of love to drive us on.

But then I realized something else. This isn't just a book about ADHD. Sure, we've talked about it a lot and it was the main reason for writing the book. But the ideas and tips here could apply to any relationship.

It doesn't matter which of you has ADHD. Or if both of you have it. Or neither of you do. This book has simply looked at smart ways of keeping a relationship full of love. Every relationship goes through ups and downs. They all have good times and bad times.

What I realized after writing this book is that there are certain tools we can use to get through the bad times and make the most of the good times. Best of all, it mostly comes down to common sense. I hope you agree that nothing in this book has been particularly difficult or complicated.

You need a sense of love to sustain the relationship and to keep you buoyed throughout the many challenges you'll experience. To reinforce that, let's review the main learning points from the book. See if you can agree that they aren't just for ADHD couples but perhaps relevant for all people in the given situations.

STRATEGIES FOR BUILDING A STRONGER RELATIONSHIP IN THE FACE OF ADHD CHALLENGES

We've looked at many and varied strategies throughout the book. The following are the parts that I most enjoyed creating and that I expect you will get the most benefit from. In some cases, I've related it to my situation with Sally. Having a reason to recall these moments helped me to put the struggle with ADHD into context.

Communication And Conflict Resolution Skills

If you're only going to carry out one thing that we've looked at here, I hope it's an improvement in your communication with your partner. Obviously, I hope you put it all into practice. But this is the area where you can get the most benefit and most satisfaction.

We looked at tips such as validation and empathy. These are excellent strategies for anyone in any type of relationship. By showing that you're in this together and that you understand your partner's struggles, you can help the communication to flow.

Techniques For Building Trust and Intimacy

This is another area where many couples let their relationship drift into dangerous waters. I know because that's exactly the situation we were in. When I left our relationship, I knew what had gone wrong. Deep down, I probably already knew what had to be done to fix it.

In the same way, I'd guess that you have an idea of what may have gone wrong and what you need to fix. This, I hope, should help you to put your thoughts in order and maybe look at your relationship in a new light,

Intimacy isn't some sort of reward that arrives after you've spent a lot of time together. It's the glue that holds you and your partner together. If you lose this then you could end up losing faith in the entire relationship. Make it a priority and set aside time to allow your physical needs to be satisfied. You won't regret it.

Setting Goals

We've looked at setting goals in a financial sense. This is a part of life we simply can't ignore. Look after your finances and it will go a long way towards giving you a better future.

However, it would be wrong to say that you only need to make financial plans. There are plenty of other plans you can make as a couple. Where do you want to travel to? Where do you want to buy your first house? Whether you want to start a family? What are dreams for the future that you've never told anyone else about?

All these things are important too. By planning for the future, you're showing your commitment. A person with ADHD tends to struggle with being too impulsive. By looking further ahead and sharing goals that they can aim for with you, you might be making a contribution to them in this area of their lives that they may not otherwise get to experience.

It's also a way of staying connected with your partner. Having a shared goal gives you something to dream about and discuss, even when times are difficult.

Self-Care

The importance of taking care of yourself is not to be overlooked. Self-care can be described as the process of putting aside enough time to look after yourself physically and mentally.

I know that having an ADHD partner can be time-consuming and draining. For both of you, this is a relationship that's going to take a lot of time and effort. That means that you can't afford to let your self-care slip.

The most effective tips for looking after yourself are usually common sense, like these:

- Exercise regularly, even if you can't dedicate time to working out as often as you'd like to.

- Embrace a healthy diet. Eating a healthy diet and drinking enough water to stay full of energy will make all the difference. Stay away from the foods that you know do you harm.

- Get enough sleep. You're probably worried and anxious about the effect that ADHD has on your relationship. This can be exhausting and you need to make an effort to follow good habits for getting enough sleep each night.

- Make time to relax. Giving yourself time to relax is going to help you feel better. Don't let each day slip by without relaxing while you do something enjoyable.

- Stay positive. Don't let the ADHD issue cause you to feel negative and frustrated. You need to stay positive if you're going to help your partner and improve your relationship.

Professional Help

Everything we've looked at here are simple tips that anyone can try. There's no intensive training course or experience needed. That means you can start making big changes to your relationship today.

But there is one area that I suggest may take more time. You might wonder whether getting professional help is worth it. It definitely is, as the right therapist can help you to see your situation in a new light. Don´t look at this as a last resort. It can help you come to terms with ADHD at any point in your relationship.

Supporting Your Partner

Let's not forget that your partner needs a huge amount of support. This is the sort of difficult situation where having someone by your side who loves and supports you makes a huge difference.

I hope that the information you've read here shows you to do this. It's something I've been through, so my aim has been to let you see what I've learned on the journey.

ADHD COUPLES

There are many challenges along the way. As a final thought, I'd like to go back over the key tips we've covered.

- Empathy and validation. These are crucial to your communication. If you've been struggling to communicate, this could be exactly what you need to sort this out.

- Take care of yourself and each other. Staying fit and healthy is going to be a huge help in getting through this.

- Avoid blaming them. Always remember that this is no one's fault. You're in it together and looking for solutions as a loving couple, and that's what matters.

I hope you've been able to relate to the points I've made and that you use this book, along with the LearnWell Community, to improve your relationship in the way I improved mine with Sally. ADHD makes it difficult to have a strong, loving relationship but it is entirely possible.

We're the living proof of that and I am certain that you and your partner can be too.

Best wishes in life and love,
Robert

REFERENCES

1. https://www.healthline.com/health/adhd/history
2. https://www.cdc.gov/ncbddd/adhd/diagnosis.html
3. https://www.mayoclinic.org/diseases-conditions/adult-adhd/symptoms-causes/syc-20350878
4. https://www.healthline.com/health/adhd/adhd-symptoms-in-girls-and-boys
5. https://intermountainhealthcare.org/blogs/topics/live-well/2017/03/busting-the-myths-about-adhd/
6. https://chadd.org/about-adhd/long-term-outcomes/
7. https://www.webmd.com/add-adhd/childhood-adhd/parenting-role-in-adhd
8. https://www.mayoclinic.org/healthy-lifestyle/stress-management/in-depth/exercise-and-stress/art-20044469
9. https://www.healthline.com/health/sleep-deprivation/effects-on-body
10. https://www.additudemag.com/cognitive-behavioral-therapy-for-adhd/
11. https://www.healthline.com/health/adhd/supplements
12. https://www.ncbi.nlm.nih.gov/pmc/articles/PMC4170184/
13. https://www.ncbi.nlm.nih.gov/pmc/articles/PMC3148992/
14. https://www.cnvc.org/sites/default/files/2018-10/CNVC-needs-inventory.pdf
15. https://www.healthline.com/health/mental-health/emotional-triggers
16. https://umatter.princeton.edu/respect/tools/communication-styles

17. https://www.cosmopolitan.com/uk/body/health/g38300011/celebrities-adhd/
18. https://www.eehealth.org/blog/2019/05/emotions-contagious/
19. https://www.healthline.com/health/emotional-needs
20. ttps://chadd.org/adhd-news/adhd-news-adults/emotions-feel-like-too-much-it-could-be-a-symptom-of-adhd/
21. https://www.adhdcentre.co.uk/adhd-emotional-dysregulation/
22. https://www.mentalhealth.org.uk/explore-mental-health/mental-health-statistics/stress-statistics
23. https://www.stress.org/daily-life
24. https://chadd.org/about-adhd/adhd-quick-facts-medication-in-adhd-treatment/
25. https://www.nbcnews.com/better/lifestyle/chore-war-how-stop-fighting-about-housework-get-cleaning-done-ncna1039916
26. https://greatspeech.com/does-adhd-affect-speech-in-adults/
27. https://www.verywellmind.com/adderall-and-emotional-detachment-why-it-happens-and-how-to-cope-6831140
28. https://www.mindbodygreen.com/articles/how-important-is-sex-in-relationships
29. https://www.ncbi.nlm.nih.gov/pmc/articles/PMC9915044/
30. https://adhdrollercoaster.org/book-club/adhd-marriage-money/
31. https://investor.vanguard.com/investor-resources-education/emergency-fund/whats-the-right-emergency-fund-amount
32. https://www.cnbc.com/select/how-money-can-build-or-break-relationships/

www.ingramcontent.com/pod-product-compliance
Lightning Source LLC
Chambersburg PA
CBHW060457080526
44584CB00015B/1456